Kristen,
Thanks for your help
with this book. You've
been a wonderful student
in several of my classes
and I hope that your
semester in Japan turns
out to be the best part
of your college years.
    Best wishes,
        Grant Hardy

THE ESTABLISHMENT OF THE HAN EMPIRE AND IMPERIAL CHINA

Greenwood Guides to Historic Events of the Ancient World

The Peloponnesian War
Lawrence Tritle

The Reign of Cleopatra
Stanley Burstein

The Decline and Fall of the Roman Empire
James W. Ermatinger

The Trojan War
Carol G. Thomas and Craig Conant

The Emperor Justinian and the Byzantine Empire
James Allan Evans

THE ESTABLISHMENT OF THE HAN EMPIRE AND IMPERIAL CHINA

Grant Hardy and
Anne Behnke Kinney

Greenwood Guides to Historic Events of the Ancient World
Bella Vivante, Series Editor

GREENWOOD PRESS
Westport, Connecticut • London

Library of Congress Cataloging-in-Publication Data

Hardy, Grant.
  The establishment of the Han empire and imperial China / Grant Hardy and Anne
Behnke Kinney
      p. cm.—(Greenwood guides to historic events of the ancient world)
    Includes bibliographical references and index.
    ISBN 0–313–32588–X (alk. paper)
    1. China—History—Han dynasty, 202 B.C.–220 A.D. I. Kinney, Anne Behnke.
II. Title. III. Series.
  DS748.H283 2005
  931'.04—dc22   2004022475

British Library Cataloguing in Publication Data is available.

Library of Congress Catalog Card Number: 2004022475
ISBN: 0–313–32588–X

First published in 2005

Greenwood Press, 88 Post Road West, Westport, CT 06881
An imprint of Greenwood Publishing Group, Inc.
www.greenwood.com

Printed in the United States of America

The paper used in this book complies with the
Permanent Paper Standard issued by the National
Information Standards Organization (Z39.48–1984).

10 9 8 7 6 5 4 3 2 1

For Heather and
Zoe Olivia

CONTENTS

Photo essay follows Chapter 5.

Series Foreword

As a professor and scholar of the ancient Greek world, I am often asked by students and scholars of other disciplines, why study antiquity? What possible relevance could human events from two, three, or more thousand years ago have to our lives today? This questioning of the continued validity of our historical past may be the offshoot of the forces shaping the history of the American people. Proud of forging a new nation out of immigrants wrenched willingly or not from their home soils, Americans have experienced a liberating headiness of separation from traditional historical demands on their social and cultural identity. The result has been a skepticism about the very validity of that historical past. Some of that skepticism is healthy and serves constructive purposes of scholarly inquiry. Questions of how, by whom, and in whose interest "history" is written are valid questions pursued by contemporary historians striving to uncover the multiple forces shaping any historical event and the multilayered social consequences that result. But the current academic focus on "presentism"—the concern with only recent events and a deliberate ignoring of premodern eras—betrays an extreme distortion of legitimate intellectual inquiry. This stress on the present seems to have deepened in the early years of the twenty-first century. The cybertechnological explosions of the preceding decades seem to have propelled us into a new cultural age requiring new rules that make the past appear all the more obsolete.

So again I ask, why study ancient cultures? In the past year, after it ousted that nation's heinous regime, the United States' occupation of Iraq has kept that nation in the forefront of the news. The land base of Iraq is ancient Mesopotamia, "the land between the rivers" of the Tigris and Euphrates, two of the four rivers in the biblical Garden of Eden (Gen. 2). Called the cradle of civilization, this area witnessed the early development of a centrally organized, hierarchical social system that utilized the new technology of writing to administer an increasingly complex state.

Is there a connection between the ancient events, literature, and art coming out of this land and contemporary events? Michael Wood, in his educational video *Iraq: The Cradle of Civilization*, produced shortly after the 1991 Gulf War, thinks so and makes this connection explicit—between the people, their way of interacting with their environment, and even the cosmological stories they create to explain and define their world.

Study of the ancient world, like study of contemporary cultures other than one's own, has more than academic or exotic value. First, study of the past seeks meaning beyond solely acquiring factual knowledge. It strives to understand the human and social dynamics that underlie any historical event and what these underlying dynamics teach us about ourselves as human beings in interaction with one another. Study of the past also encourages deeper inquiry than what appears to some as the "quaint" observation that this region of current and recent conflict could have served as a biblical ideal or as a critical marker in the development of world civilizations. In fact, these apparently quaint dimensions can serve as the hook that piques our interest into examining the past and discovering what it may have to say to us today. Not an end in itself, the knowledge forms the bedrock for exploring deeper meanings.

Consider, for example, the following questions. What does it mean that three major world religions—Judaism, Christianity, and Islam—developed out of the ancient Mesopotamian worldview? In this view, the world, and hence its gods, were seen as being in perpetual conflict with one another and with the environment, and death was perceived as a matter of despair and desolation. What does it mean that Western forms of thinking derive from the particular intellectual revolution of archaic Greece that developed into what is called rational discourse, ultimately systematized by Aristotle in the fourth century B.C.E.? How does this thinking, now fundamental to Western discourse, shape how we see the world and ourselves, and how we interact with one another? And how does it affect our ability, or lack thereof, to communicate intelligibly with people with differently framed cultural perceptions? What, ultimately, do we gain from being aware of the origin and development of these fundamental features of our thinking and beliefs?

In short, knowing the past is essential for knowing ourselves in the present. Without an understanding of where we came from, and the journey we took to get where we are today, we cannot understand why we think or act the way we do. Nor, without an understanding of historical development, are we in a position to make the kinds of constructive changes necessary to advance as a society. Awareness of the past gives us the resources necessary to make comparisons between our contemporary world and past times. It is from those comparisons that we can assess both the advances we have made as human societies and those aspects that can still benefit from change. Hence, knowledge of the past is crucial for shaping our individual and social identities, providing us with the resources to make intelligent, aware, and informed decisions for the future.

All ancient societies, whether significant for the evolution of Western ideas and values, or whether they developed largely separate from the cultures that more directly influenced Western civilization, such as China, have important lessons to teach us. For fundamentally they all address questions that have faced every human individual and every human society that has existed. Because ancient civilizations erected great monuments of themselves in stone, writings, and the visual arts— all enduring material evidence—we can view how these ancient cultures dealt with many of the same questions we face today. And we learn the consequences of the actions taken by people in other societies and times that, ideally, should help us as we seek solutions to contemporary issues. Thus it was that President John F. Kennedy wrote of his reliance upon Thucydides' treatment of the devastating war between the ancient Greek city-states of Athens and Sparta (see the volume on the Peloponnesian War) in his study of exemplary figures, *Profiles in Courage*.

This series seeks to fulfill this goal both collectively and in the individual volumes. The individual volumes examine key events, trends, and developments in world history in ancient times that are central to the secondary school and lower-level undergraduate history curriculum and that form standard topics for student research. From a vast field of potential subjects, these selected topics emerged after consultations with scholars, educators, and librarians. Each book in the series can be described as a "library in a book." Each one presents a chronological timeline and an initial factual overview of its subject, three to five topical essays that examine the subject from diverse perspectives and for its various consequences, a concluding essay providing current perspectives on the event, biographies of key players, a selection of primary documents, illustrations, a glossary, and an index. The concept of the series is to provide ready-reference materials that include a quick, in-depth examination of the topic and insightful guidelines for interpretive analysis, suitable for student research and designed to stimulate critical thinking. The authors are all scholars of the topic in their fields, selected both on the basis of their expertise and for their ability to bring their scholarly knowledge to a wider audience in an engaging and clear way. In these regards, this series follows the concept and format of the Greenwood Guides to Historic Events of the Twentieth Century, the Fifteenth to Nineteenth Centuries, and the Medieval World.

All the works in this series deal with historical developments in early ancient civilizations, almost invariably postdating the emergence of writing and of hierarchical dynastic social structures. Perhaps only incidentally do they deal with what historians call the Paleolithic ("Old Stone Age") periods, from about 25,000 B.C.E. onward, eras characterized by nomadic, hunting-gathering societies, or the Neolithic ("New Stone Age"), the period of the earliest development of agriculture and hence settled societies, one of the earliest dating to about 7000 B.C.E. at Çatal Höyük in south-central Turkey.

The earliest dates covered by the books in this series are the fourth to second millennia B.C.E. for the building of the Pyramids in Egypt, and the examination of the Trojan War and the Bronze Age civilizations of the eastern Mediterranean. Most volumes deal with events in the first millennium B.C.E. to the early centuries of the first millennium C.E. Some treat the development of civilizations, such as the rise of the Han Empire in China, or the separate volumes on the rise and on the decline and fall of the Roman Empire. Some highlight major personalities and their empires, such as the volumes on Cleopatra VII of Ptolemaic Egypt or Justinian and the beginnings of the Byzantine Empire in eastern Greece and Constantinople (Istanbul). Three volumes examine the emergence in antiquity of religious movements that form major contemporary world systems of belief—Judaism, Buddhism, and Christianity. (Islam is being treated in the parallel Medieval World series.) And two volumes examine technological developments, one on the building of the Pyramids and one on other ancient technologies.

Each book examines the complexities of the forces shaping the development of its subject and the historical consequences. Thus, for example, the volume on the fifth-century B.C.E. Greek Peloponnesian War explores the historical causes of the war, the nature of the combatants' actions, and how these reflect the thinking of the period. A particular issue, which may seem strange to some or timely to others, is how a city like Athens, with its proto-democratic political organization and its outstanding achievements in architecture, sculpture, painting, drama, and philosophy, could engage in openly imperialist policies of land conquest and of vicious revenge against any who countered them. Rather than trying to gloss over the contradictions that emerge, these books conscientiously explore whatever tensions arise in the ancient material, both to portray more completely the ancient event and to highlight the fact that no historical occurrence is simply determined. Sometimes societies that we admire in some ways—such as the artistic achievements and democratic political experiments of ancient Athens—may prove deeply troublesome in other ways—such as what we see as their reprehensible conduct in war and in brutal subjection of other Greek communities. Consequently, the reader is empowered to make informed, well-rounded judgments on the events and actions of the major players.

We offer this series as an invitation to explore the past in various ways. We anticipate that from its volumes the reader will gain a better appreciation of the historical events and forces that shaped the lives of our ancient forebears and that continue to shape our thinking, values, and actions today. However remote in time and culture these ancient civilizations may at times appear, ultimately they show us that the questions confronting human beings of any age are timeless and that the examples of the past can provide valuable insights into our understanding of the present and the future.

Bella Vivante
University of Arizona

PREFACE

For traditional Chinese scholars, the Han dynasty (202 B.C.E.–220 C.E.) was only one in a long series of Chinese dynasties. It had been preceded by the Shang and Zhou dynasties, and was eventually followed by the Tang and Song dynasties. From the mid-second-millennium B.C.E. to 1912 C.E. there were ten major dynasties—periods of time in which a single family controlled China—along with dozens of regimes that claimed the title but only ruled a portion of China. Yet from the perspective of world history there was a dramatic shift that occurred in the Han. Early Chinese dynasties were small kingdoms in North China held together by family connections and loose feudal ties. The Han dynasty, by contrast, was an empire that conquered most of the area we think of today as China, from Korea in the north to Vietnam in the south, and from Tibet to the Pacific Ocean. The Han even controlled the Silk Road that stretched deep into Central Asia. As an empire, it ruled over peoples who spoke different languages, worshiped different gods, and followed different customs, but gradually the cultural traditions of North China, including its philosophy, family structure, political organization, and writing system, were accepted throughout the territory of present-day China. Its cultural transformation was much more thorough than that of the Roman Empire—another empire that conquered vast territories at about the same time—and this is one reason that China exists today as a unified cultural and political entity while Rome is gone forever.

The Han dynasty, which we will unambiguously refer to as the Han Empire throughout this book, started it all. The story of how it came into being and how it laid the foundation for later Chinese regimes is one of the most significant tales in world history. The establishment of the Han Empire was actually a two-step process that began with the short-lived Qin dynasty (221–207 B.C.E.), which ended centuries of warfare between rival kingdoms by forcefully taking control of continental East Asia. (The name Qin, sometimes spelled as Ch'in, is the source for our word "China.") The First Emperor, as he styled himself, centralized his command by completely remaking society. His attempts proved to be too much change, too fast, and his government collapsed within fourteen years. The first ruler of the Han Empire, Liu Bang, held on to power by combining practices of the Qin regime with elements of the ancient political arrangement that the Qin had brutally destroyed. In the end, Liu's successors managed to create a government that proved much more stable and enduring than either the feudal system of ancient China or the harsh bureaucracy of the Qin.

We will examine this process of creation from a number of perspectives, in five chapters. The first offers a straightforward political history in which we recount the major players, their rise to power, significant battles, and court intrigues. The second chapter looks at empire building as a balance between the central government and regional authorities. It is here that we will see how emperors acted decisively to exert greater control over a huge region and how they developed specific policies to unite diverse groups within a single culture. The third explores the material basis of empire—that is, how new tools and techniques boosted agricultural production enough to support large, well-equipped armies as well as an extensive bureaucracy. Empires, in the end, are always based on agricultural surplus and military power. The fourth chapter examines the effects of this new form of political organization on social life. What did these momentous changes mean for individuals, and particularly for the women and children who are so often overlooked in traditional historical writing? The last chapter is an interpretive essay that briefly glances at cross-cultural comparisons and the long-term consequences of the Han Empire both for China and for the rest of the world. Finally, a series of twenty biographies and fourteen primary sources rounds out the picture. The focus of this book will be on the Qin dynasty and early Han Empire through the reign of Emperor Wu (147–87 B.C.E.).

We hope that by telling the story of the founding of the Han in several different ways—as political history, institutional history, technological history, social history, and comparative history, and through biographies and ancient documents—readers will gain a sense of the richness and diversity of this event. Our basic source for this account is a single text, the *Shiji* (Records of the Grand Historian), a history written by Sima Qian about 90 B.C.E. His was the first comprehensive history of China and it was truly an impressive achievement (indeed, one of the most notable accomplishments of Han culture). Chinese scholars have long supplemented his record with other early texts, but the twentieth century brought to China new approaches to the study of the past, and in particular the science of archaeology. Every year brings new and exciting archaeological discoveries that date back to the Han Empire; sometimes these recently excavated finds have dramatically confirmed Sima's narrative and sometimes they have challenged it. We will bring together as much evidence as we can within this limited volume, but we will conclude with a list of specialized resources that students can consult for more detailed information.

Even during the Han, China was an immense country with an enormous population. The enormous scope of the empire presents difficulties for any brief historical account that by necessity can focus only on a few key individuals and concepts. It's not as if people woke up one morning in 202 B.C.E. and said, "Well that's it; the course of human history has been changed forever." The significance of any historical event equaling the magnitude of the founding of the Han and the establishment of Imperial China becomes evident only over the course of several centuries and millions of lives. At best, we can hope to present the basic outlines of a momentous transition that we are still trying to understand, but which nevertheless continues to shape the world in which we live.

I would like to thank the students who were in my spring 2004 special-topics course on the founding of the Han dynasty. They read drafts of most of the material that follows, and their criticisms and suggestions made this a much better book. My colleagues at the Southeast Early China Roundtable also offered useful advice, and as always, I owe a great debt to my wife, Heather.

Grant Hardy

I would like to thank colleagues of the Warring States Working Group for their many useful suggestions and references, as well as Sarah Wells and Chris Jessee of the University of Virginia for their assistance with maps and tables. I am also grateful for the loving support of my husband, Dan, and the great blessing of my precious daughter, Zoe, to whom I have dedicated this book.

Anne Behnke Kinney

A NOTE ON CHINESE TRANSLITERATION, PRONUNCIATION, NAMES, DATES, AND SOURCES

The study of Chinese history presents several challenges for Western students from the outset. First, the Chinese language is very different from English or any of the Indo-European languages like Spanish, French, or German that Americans commonly study. To begin with, written Chinese is based on characters rather than an alphabet. This means that Chinese children learning to read must master thousands of characters that range from a single line to over thirty separate brush strokes. It is a difficult task, but perhaps it is not unlike English speakers spending years learning how to spell English words correctly. Over the last couple of centuries, many systems have been devised to render Chinese characters into alphabetic form so that foreigners can write out the pronunciation of Chinese words and names. Two of the most commonly used schemes are the Wade-Giles system and Pinyin. The latter has gained dominance in the last few decades since its adoption by the People's Republic of China and will be used in this book. Nevertheless, students doing research in libraries will frequently encounter names and book titles in Wade-Giles. As an example, the Chinese name 司馬遷 can be transliterated as both "Ssu-ma Ch'ien" (Wade-Giles) and "Sima Qian" (Pinyin), but the Chinese historian referred to is one and the same. In the biographies, names will be spelled using both styles of transliteration.

Chinese includes sounds that English does not have, and these account for some of the odder looking combinations of letters. The following equivalences will help in pronouncing Chinese names and terms in this volume:

Pinyin	English
c	ts
q	ch
x	hs (close to a soft sh)
z	dz (as in pizza)
zh	j (as in jump)

In an effort to help introduce students to Pinyin—which can seem intimidating with its *q*'s and *x*'s—pronunciation suggestions are provided in parentheses at the first occurrence of important names. These spellings in parenthesis are not from a standard, linguistically-correct romanization system; rather, they offer a rough guide that matches sounds with letter combinations that will be more familiar to English-speaking readers. For example, the Pinyin name "Liu Bang" might be followed by "(*Leo Bahng*)." Students should try to pronounce the names as they read. Although Chinese sounds can be confusing, pronouncing the names as one reads is the only way to keep the cast of characters and stories straight.

Chinese names appear in reverse order from English names; that is, the family name comes first. So Liu Bang's family name is "Liu," and "Bang" is his given name. Unfortunately, prominent Chinese individuals are often given several names over the course of their lifetimes, so Liu Bang can also be referred to as Liu Ji and Gaozu (a title meaning "Exalted Ancestor"), as well as the Lord of Pei and the King of Han. In this book we will refer to individuals by a single name, though some alternative names and titles will be included in the biographies.

In Chinese history there was no universal, linear system of dates like our B.C.E./C.E. continuum. In this book we will use B.C.E.—before the common era—instead of B.C., and C.E.—common era—instead of A.D., in keeping with contemporary scholarly usage, which prefers these religiously neutral terms. In premodern China, events were dated from the beginning of each ruler's reign. Thus in pre-imperial times, each state had its own calendar that began with year one for each new ruler. For example, Confucius, a native of the state of Lu, was born in the twenty-second year of Duke Xiang of Lu, a year equivalent to the twenty-first year of King

Ling of Zhou and the third year of Duke Zhuang in the state of Qi. The situation got easier after China was unified, because the calendar was then established according to the reign of one emperor rather than a multitude of kings. But Emperor Wu decided to start the calendar over several times during his fifty-four-year reign, and later emperors followed this practice of dividing their years on the throne into shorter "reign periods." One result of all this is that there is some confusion about the dates of the Han dynasty. In this book we will begin it at 202 B.C.E., when Liu Bang was proclaimed emperor. However, Chinese sources date events from the start of his taking the title of King of Han—something that happened in 206 B.C.E.—and this earlier year is often cited as the beginning of the dynasty.

The history of the Han Empire is known to us through two major sources—the *Shiji* (Records of the Grand Historian) by Sima Qian, written about 90 B.C.E., and the *Han shu* (Book of the Han), an adaptation and expansion of Sima Qian's work composed about 90 C.E. by Ban Gu and completed by his sister Ban Zhao. The *Shiji* presents all of Chinese history in 130 chapters, divided as follows:

10 basic annals recounting earlier dynasties and the reigns of individual emperors in the Qin and Han Empires

10 chronological tables correlating major events in the feudal states and Han Empire

8 treatises dealing with ritual, music, pitch-pipes, the calendar, astronomy, state sacrifices, waterways, and economics

30 hereditary houses devoted to the feudal lords

70 biographies, including group biographies of assassins, scholars, harsh officials, and merchants, as well as chapters on foreign peoples.

The *Han shu* recounts only the first half of the Han dynasty, but it adopts a similar format with twelve annals, eight tables, ten treatises, and seventy biographies. Much of the information in the *Han shu* about the founding of the dynasty is borrowed directly from Sima Qian. Other information about the Han Empire comes from the writings of Han officials and philosophers, and in recent years from archaeological discoveries. These newly discovered resources are usually derived from tombs that contain material goods and sometimes texts written on thin strips of bamboo. Artwork from the Han can also provide clues about life at that time.

MAJOR CHINESE DYNASTIES AND ERAS

Xia dynasty (c. 2070–c. 1600 B.C.E.)
Shang dynasty (c. 1570–1045 B.C.E.)
Zhou dynasty (1045–256 B.C.E.)
      Western Zhou (1045–771 B.C.E.)
      Eastern Zhou (770–256 B.C.E.)
         Spring and Autumn Era (722–481 B.C.E.)
         Warring States Era (403–221 B.C.E.)
Qin dynasty (221–207 B.C.E.)
Han dynasty (202 B.C.E.–220 C.E.)
Six Dynasties Era (including the Three Kingdoms, the Jin dynasty, the Six Dynasties in the South, and the Sixteen Kingdoms in the North) (220–589)
Sui dynasty (589–618)
Tang dynasty (618–907)
Five Dynasties Era (907–960)
Song dynasty (960–1279)
Yuan dynasty (1264–1368)
Ming dynasty (1368–1644)
Qing dynasty (1644–1911)
Republic of China (1912–1949)
People's Republic of China (1949–present)

Early Han Rulers

Liu Bang (also known as Gaozu, "Exalted Ancestor")
  Born a commoner
  King of Han in 206
  Emperor from 202 to 195
  Died between 50 and 60 years of age

Emperor Hui (Liu Ying)
  Son of Liu Bang and Empress Lü
  Emperor from 195 to 188 (began rule at age 15)

Empress Lü
  Wife of Liu Bang
  Ruled as regent for two child emperors (said to be sons of Emperor Hui)
  In power from 188 to 180

Emperor Wen (Liu Heng)
  Son of Liu Bang and consort Bo
  King of Dai in 196
  Emperor from 180 to 157

Emperor Jing (Liu Qi)
  Son of Emperor Wen and Empress Dou
  Emperor from 157 to 141

Emperor Wu (Liu Che)
> Son of Emperor Jing and Empress Wang
> King of Jiaotong in 153
> Heir apparent from 150 to 141
> Emperor from 141 to 87 (began rule at age 15)

(All dates are B.C.E.; all the above ruled until their deaths.)

CHRONOLOGY OF EVENTS

(All dates are B.C.E.)

1045	Founding of the Zhou dynasty.
722	Beginning of the Spring and Autumn Era.
551	Birth of Confucius (551–479).
481	End of Spring and Autumn Era.
403	Beginning of Warring States Era.
361	Arrival in Qin of Legalist reformer Shang Yang (d. 338).
350–338	Major reforms in Qin.
334	Duke of Qi is the first feudal lord to take the title of "king."
256	Qin conquers the state of Zhou and ends the Zhou dynasty.
246	Zheng becomes king of the state of Qin.
230–221	Qin destroys the last six feudal kingdoms—Hann (230), Zhao (228), Wei (225), Chu (223), Yan (222), and Qi (221); end of the Warring States Era.
221	Founding of the Qin dynasty; King Zheng takes the title First Emperor.

213	Li Si is chancellor; the burning of the books.
210	First Emperor dies; Second Emperor comes to the throne.
209	Chen She rebels, along with many others.
208	Li Si executed; Liu Bang joins with Xiang Yu.
207	Death of the Second Emperor; Zhao Gao executed; fall of the Qin dynasty.
206	Xiang Yu establishes a confederacy of nineteen kingdoms with himself as the preeminent "hegemon-king"; Liu Bang is appointed king of Han; Liu conquers the three kings assigned to the old capital region of Qin and takes possession of that area; other kings also attack each other.
205	Liu Bang leads his troops east where they are defeated by Xiang Yu. Liu barely escapes in a storm.
204	With the help of Xiao He and Han Xin, Liu is able to raise another army, but he is again defeated. Again he barely escapes.
203	Liu rewards his general Han Xin by making him king of Qi; Liu and Xiang agree to divide China in two, with Liu taking the western half and Xiang the east.
202	Liu attacks Xiang, who commits suicide. Liu claims the title of emperor and establishes the Han dynasty. One-third of the empire is organized into commanderies; two-thirds are divided among ten kingdoms.
202–195	Reign of Emperor Gaozu (Liu Bang).
200	Liu leads an unsuccessful campaign against the Xiongnu nomads; he puts down the first of several rebellions in the kingdoms.
198	The Chinese sign a peace treaty with the Xiongnu.

196	Officials are ordered to nominate worthy candidates for the bureaucracy.
195	Liu Bang dies. The next rulers include his son and two grandsons, but since they are all young, the real power is wielded by Empress Lü, Liu's widow.
195–188	Reign of Emperor Hui.
191	Books banned by First Emperor are again allowed to circulate.
188–180	Rule of Empress Lü (as regent and dowager empress).
180	Empress Lü dies; her clan is massacred and power remains with the Liu family.
180–157	Reign of Emperor Wen.
167	Punishment by mutilation is abolished.
157–141	Reign of Emperor Jing.
154	Seven kingdoms rebel against the central government and are crushed.
145	Senior officials in the kingdoms are appointed by the central government.
141–87	Reign of Emperor Wu.
136	The emperor sponsors "Erudite Scholars" for each of the Five Confucian Classics.
133	The first of several major offenses is launched against the Xiongnu.
127	A decree requires kings and marquises to divide their territories equally among all their sons.
124	The Imperial Academy is founded with fifty students studying the Confucian Classics.
120	A series of major military campaigns begins that will take Chinese armies into Burma, Vietnam,

Korea, and Central Asia over the next twenty years, resulting in a tremendous expansion of the Han Empire.

119 Government monopolies of salt and iron are established.

114 The Bureau of Music is created.

112 The central government confiscates over one hundred marquisates in a single year.

106 Regional inspectors are appointed.

104 The calendar is reformed and the reign period "Grand Beginning" is proclaimed.

100 By this time most of China is organized into some eighty-four commanderies; there are still eighteen kingdoms, but they are smaller and much weaker than before.

c. 90 Sima Qian writes his history, in 130 chapters.

CHAPTER 1

THE ESTABLISHMENT OF THE HAN EMPIRE: AN OVERVIEW

On February 28, 202 B.C.E., over three hundred nobles and generals gathered on the north bank of the Fan River to proclaim Liu Bang (pronounced *Leo Bahng*) the first emperor of the Han (*Hahn*) dynasty.[1] They had little idea of what the future might bring, but they certainly hoped that a new dynasty would mean the end of war. For five years China had been torn apart by civil war between the forces of Liu Bang and Xiang Yu (*Shee-ong You*). This struggle had followed the collapse of the repressive Qin (*Cheen*) dynasty, which itself had only offered fourteen years of respite from five centuries of nearly constant warfare. Tens of thousands of men had died in battle, traditional Chinese culture had been turned upside down, and the people were exhausted. Perhaps stability had finally come.

In fact, the Han dynasty would last for over four hundred years, easily rivaling its contemporary on the other side of Eurasia—the Roman Empire—in terms of territory, military might, cultural sophistication, and population (both had about 60 million people). (See the volumes in the Greenwood Guides to Historic Events on the rise of the Roman Empire and the decline and fall of the Roman Empire.) Equally important, the methods of government developed at that time would serve as the basis for Imperial China—the sequence of dynasties that would carry China into the twentieth century, when the last emperor of China lost his throne in 1911 C.E. Although there were many changes over the two thousand years of Imperial China, there were remarkable continuities as well, and Chinese civilization ranks as one of the most successful social systems in human history.

As Liu Bang took the title of emperor on that chilly February day, everyone in attendance must have thought about the history of that office, and what accepting it might mean. The Chinese had long believed in an impersonal, moral force they called Heaven. With the approval, or mandate, of Heaven, a king could gain power and rule, but when his descendants became corrupt and oblivious to the suffering of the common people, Heaven would withdraw its mandate and bestow it upon another family who were thereby authorized to lead a revolt. The last time Heaven had unambiguously chosen a ruler was nearly eight hundred years earlier, with the founding of the Zhou (Joe) dynasty. But the last ruler of that line had been overthrown some fifty-four years earlier in 256, and there had been chaos ever since. The First Emperor of the Qin dynasty had unified China in 221, but he had done so through sheer military force and had not justified his actions by claiming the Mandate. In fact, his scholars had advocated an entirely different model of political change based on Five Phases—Earth, Wood, Metal, Fire, and Water—that naturally overcame one another in turn. He claimed that his armies had conquered the Zhou dynasty, associated with Fire, by the awesome power of Water, and he invented the new title of "Emperor" to reflect his unprecedented power as the solitary ruler sitting at the apex of a centralized, bureaucratic empire. But his presumption now looked laughable in light of his short-lived reign.

Could Liu Bang, who had begun his life as a peasant, be the next recipient of Heaven's mandate? Would he too rule by the power of Water or would he adopt his own patron phase? Could he even claim the title of "Emperor"? Within weeks of the death of his rival Xiang Yu, Liu's advisors were urging him to make himself an emperor. In good Chinese fashion, he refused three times, saying, "I have heard that the title of emperor can only be held by those who are worthy. It is not something that can be maintained by empty words and vain speeches. I dare not accept the position of emperor." In the end, however, he sat on the throne (as he had wanted all along) with the excuse that he was doing so "for the good of the country."[2]

Liu's first act as emperor was to appoint seven of his followers as deputy kings (this formal recognition of their local authority was probably one reason they encouraged him to become emperor), and then, as the great historian Sima Qian (Sue-ma Chyen) noted in a particularly resonant phrase, "All under Heaven was at peace." But this was not the end of the story; indeed, it was not really the beginning either. The Han represented a continuation of many earlier practices—especially those of the Qin dynasty, which it simultaneously imitated and reviled—and there were also innovations over the next century that made the Han dynasty the model of imperial rule throughout Chinese history. In telling the story of how all this came about, the place to begin is in the last, dark days of the Zhou dynasty.

THE LATE ZHOU (722–256 B.C.E.)

By the sixth century, the Zhou dynasty was beginning to falter. According to traditional sources, its beginning was glorious, starting about 1045 when King Wu (Woo) claimed the Mandate of Heaven, ousted the wicked last king of the Shang dynasty, and established a new regime. Finding that his kingdom was too large to govern by himself, he divided it into smaller territories and appointed local rulers whom he allowed to run their own lands as they saw fit, so long as they provided him with military and financial assistance on request. Of course, the people he trusted enough to make dukes (basically junior kings) were his relatives, and he had a lot of them. In addition, as new territories were brought into the Chinese cultural sphere, new states were created, and the kings of Zhou made sure the rulers of those regions were bound to the royal house by marriage ties and ritual oaths of allegiance. By the beginning of the eighth century, there were some two hundred states, most fairly small.

This system, similar to the feudalism of medieval Europe, worked well enough for several centuries, but as kingdoms were passed from generation to generation, the ties of kinship weakened, the kings of Zhou were no longer able to enforce order, and states began to compete with one another for resources and for territory. "Compete" is actually a euphemism for warfare, and the later Zhou dynasty was characterized by incessant, bloody fighting as states attempted to destroy or annex each other. At the beginning of the Spring and Autumn Era (722–481; named for a history of the state of Lu that organized events by seasons and years), there were still some one hundred and seventy states, but by the fifth century, unrelenting warfare had reduced their number to about forty. The aptly named Warring States Era (403–221) started with seven major states and ended with one, when the state of Qin finally brought all of

China under its control. Over the last five centuries of the Zhou dynasty, four out of every five years saw warfare between major states.

As competition became more intense, the old patterns of aristocratic interactions were shattered. There were assassinations, murders, coups, and even patricides, as over-eager princes killed their fathers. Noble warriors who used to regard battle as an elegant game, an opportunity to show off their valor and virtue (sometimes by granting concessions to their distinguished opponents), now slaughtered each other mercilessly, and they could even be killed by peasants armed with newly invented crossbows (see Figure 1). Treaties could not be relied on without an exchange of hostages, and sometimes not even then. The old ceremonies were still used—for instance, treaties were still sealed by rulers killing a bull and smearing its blood on their lips while swearing to the gods that they would uphold its provisions—but no one cared for the old gods anymore (they were, after all, the patron gods and ancestors of the very much weakened royal house of Zhou), and people began to speak of "breaking an oath while the blood is still wet on the lips." States lied to each other, double-crossed each other, negotiated secret treaties, and made and dissolved alliances with dizzying speed.

Rulers who worried about preserving their states, the sacrifices to their ancestors, and even their own lives started looking around for help. In this way, the breakdown of the old feudal order brought a surprising degree of social mobility as clever, eloquent men wandered from state to state, looking for a ruler who would put their ideas into practice, and rulers welcomed anyone who could promise them some advantage over their foes. The search for political, social, and economic stability fueled the creation of the "hundred schools of philosophy," and there was no end to the proposals that these wandering debaters put forward. Some were agriculturalists, who claimed new techniques for increasing the farm yields crucial to supporting large armies in the field; others knew how to construct canals; and still others were military strategists (the most famous of these was Sunzi [or Sun Tzu, *Swun-zuh*], whose *Art of War* can still be found today in most American bookstores). There were cosmologists who promised to reveal how to harness the forces of nature, logicians who analyzed argumentation itself, and even some who suggested that what the world really needed was more love (they did not last very long). Among these many competing philosophies, three schools of thought stand out as particularly significant: Confucianism, Daoism, and Legalism.

Three Philosophies

Confucius (551–479) considered himself a failure in life. Tradition has it that his pleas for employment were rejected by some seventy different rulers. When he failed to gain office, he became a teacher, and the ideas he developed were later widely adopted in China. Basically, he thought that the problems of his age—increasing violence and the breakup of society—could be countered with a return to the morality of the past, by which he meant the aristocratic ways of the early Zhou dynasty. He urged his students to study ancient history and literature, and he felt that if a ruler lived according to high ethical standards, the people would naturally follow his example. Confucius taught the importance of ritual and music in shaping moral sensibilities, and he advocated a benevolent sort of hierarchical social order. When the Duke of Qi asked him about government, he replied, "Let rulers be rulers, ministers be ministers, fathers fathers, and sons sons" (*Analects*, 12:11). The idea was that if everyone knew their place in society and acted in accordance with their position, things would run smoothly. Confucius believed that filial piety—respect for parents—was the foundation of a well-ordered society. If, for example, every father acted as a true father—caring for the welfare of his children; protecting, educating, and supporting them—and every son showed proper respect and obedience, families would be more stable and successful, and as each family observed these principles, the entire state would be transformed. Similarly, rulers and ministers should work together in a relationship that, though unequal, was nevertheless characterized by generosity and mutual concern (see Document 1).[3]

Laozi (or Lao Tzu, *Lau-zuh*; fourth century B.C.E.) saw the same social problems, but his answer was to return to the Dao (or Tao, *Dow*)—often translated as "the Way." The Dao is a bit hard to describe since Laozi taught that it was beyond words, but it acts according to natural principles and encompasses all opposites in a complementary whole (this is the concept behind the famous circular yin/yang symbol). So although we tend to judge things as being weak or strong, hard or soft, desirable or repugnant, from the perspective of nature these artificial, human distinctions don't mean much. For instance, gold and dirt are both natural products and both have their uses, but because we think that gold is more valuable, people are willing to lie and steal and even murder to get it (even though it would be impossible to grow crops in a field of gold). If people could ignore such common value judgments, everyone would be happier. As Laozi wrote in the *Daodejing* (or Tao Te Ching, *Dow-duh-jeeng*), the best society would be one made up of small villages whose inhabitants were basically content with what they had. It is desire and ambition that get us into trouble, and they are hardly ever worth it. Even more strikingly, Laozi suggests that many of the distinctions that humans make are illusory. Thus water appears soft and weak, but for wearing away mountains and digging canyons, there is nothing stronger. And opposites always come in pairs, so that when we praise someone as being beautiful, we are also implying that everyone who looks different is ugly. So also, Laozi complains that whenever the Confucians emphasized a virtue, they were also highlighting a vice. For example, he felt that the only reason people spoke so much about filial piety was because the lack of respect for parents was already a significant problem. Some listeners might respond, "You mean, not everyone obeys their parents? There's an idea!" In political terms, the best government is one that does not do much, because trying to change things too quickly will always bring a backlash of resentment.

These two philosophies have been very influential in China, and most Chinese have traditionally subscribed to both Confucianism and Daoism, at least to some degree. When times are good and hard work seems to pay off, Confucianism provides direction and encouragement to make things even better. But when times are bad and the government is corrupt, Daoism functions as a sort of safety valve, an ideology that allows withdrawal from public life when the required compromises to one's integrity become intolerable. Talented individuals are then free to pursue a simpler way of living that preserves their life, dignity, and peace of mind. To summarize, Confucianism is associated with hierarchy, order, social responsibility, service, and conformity. It is moralistic, activist, and serious. Daoism, on the other hand, values individualism, freedom, non-conformity, nature, retirement, wit, and mysticism. But Confucius and Laozi were not exactly opposites, since they shared many assumptions. They both rejected competitive strife, they were suspicious of attempts to pin down ideas in exact language, and they believed that an intuitive, spontaneous sort of harmony would naturally arise from their principles. There were others thinkers, however, who saw both philosophies as hopelessly idealistic.

The Legalists had ideas that were much more practical. You don't motivate people with vague concepts of morality or visions of a simpler world; you get them to do what you want through punishments and rewards. Legalist scholars would approach an anxious ruler and rather than saying "you first need to shape up your own life" (as did Confucians) or "relax and don't worry so much" (the Daoist line), they would suggest that if they were allowed to set up the laws of a state, the ruler could enjoy himself while the country pretty much ran itself. Laws, they argued, should be objective—quantifiable, if possible—applied equally, widely publicized, and strict. If a ruler wanted his people to fight hard in battle, he should offer a reward—say, a piece of gold for each enemy head the soldier brought in. In fact, in the Legalist state of Qin, one way to get ahead was precisely "getting a head." It might be a gruesome method of accounting, but it had the advantage of being clear-cut and easily administered. And family background was irrelevant; whether someone's father was a general or a peasant, four heads were worth four pieces of gold. On the other hand, running away in battle would be punishable by death. If the laws were consistently and forcefully applied, people could be made to do almost anything.

Legalists were often regarded as the villains of Chinese philosophy because they taught techniques of government that relied on raw power and came with no moral justifications. They could make people do whatever the ruler wanted—good or bad—and most rulers were interested in success in war. Legalists therefore increased the power of the state, and they disdained history and philosophy as a waste of time. The most successful of these Legalist advisers was Lord Shang in the state of Qin.

The State of Qin

Shang Yang (*Shahng Yahng;* d. 338) was originally from the state of Wei (*Way*). Unable to secure a position there, he traveled to Qin in 361 and, through a series of interviews, gained the trust of the ruler, who permitted him to reform the laws. Lord Shang organized the people into groups of five and ten families and made them all share responsibility if any one of them broke the law. This method of mutual responsibility was used as a means of social control, and as with much Legalist policy, the concern was efficiency rather than justice or fairness. Failure to report a crime was punishable by death, and turning in a wrongdoer was generously rewarded. A new system of official ranks was implemented, and families could increase their status—which included rights to land, titles, tax breaks, slaves, and certain styles of clothing—only through military achievements and agricultural production. Noble families, if they failed in battle, would be demoted, and even the heir apparent was punished when he broke the law (actually, this proved too dangerous for Shang Yang, so the prince's tutor was punished instead). The country was divided into thirty-one districts with magistrates appointed by the ruler, while taxes—paid in both labor and goods—were regularized and sent directly to the central government. Land, no longer monopolized by the nobility, could be bought and sold, and the state actively encouraged agriculture by sponsoring irrigation projects, discriminating against merchants, and double taxing households with adult sons at home who could be establishing farms of their own.

Before this time, Qin had been like other Chinese feudal states, in which a coalition of powerful families controlled large tracts of land and the peasants who lived on them. Lord Shang established a direct relationship between the ruler and the commoners, and in so doing, he destroyed the hereditary power of the aristocracy. It was a radical reform that was probably only possible because Qin had vigorously expanded and encouraged peasants—including non-Chinese peoples and farmers from other states—to settle in the new territories where noble families had less control. In these areas, the challenge of establishing a new social order was not as formidable as it would have been in regions closer to the Chinese heartland, where aristocratic privilege held sway. Other states had experimented with similar measures—written law codes, official ranks, regular taxes, and universal military service—but nowhere were they applied as systematically or as forcefully as in Qin. Indeed, Qin was at the forefront of replacing aristocratic rule with a professionalized, bureaucratic administration.

The results of Lord Shang's reforms were mixed. For him personally, they were disastrous. It is dangerous to change things too fast (as the Daoists had warned), and many powerful people were resentful, including the heir apparent. When the king of Qin died and the heir came into the throne, Shang Yang was accused of treason and he went into hiding, only to discover that because of his own laws, no one would take him in. He tried unsuccessfully to flee abroad and then, in desperation, led his few followers in an attack on the government. He was killed, his body was torn apart by chariots, and his entire family was executed.

On the other hand, the state of Qin had enjoyed prosperity and domestic tranquillity under the new laws, and many of Lord Shang's policies continued after his death. When Qin began to defeat its neighbors decisively, other states took notice and adopted policies that increased the power of their own rulers. One of the main losers in these shifts of authority was the house of Zhou; the old days when the king of Zhou appointed dukes as heads of subordinate states was long gone. New families had seized power in various states and owed little to the Zhou, who in any case had no real military power. In fact, the relatively small state of Zhou was now dwarfed by its vassal states, some of which were growing into superpower status. In 334 the ruler of Qi (*Chee*), a duke, defied tradition and began to call himself "king." Within a decade, the leaders of all the other major states claimed the same title for themselves. Fierce fighting continued for another century, with states sometimes joining forces in an attempt to stop Qin, and sometimes fighting among themselves.

The third century was a time of dramatic change across China as states scrambled to keep up with their neighbors, realizing that survival was only possible for strong, centralized kingdoms. As military tactics shifted to common foot soldiers, rulers needed new ways to reach down to the lowest levels of society to draw on the military potential of all their subjects. The expansion of cultivated lands was seen crucial to success, and governments invested heavily in massive irrigation projects such as dams and canals (the "investment" in this case was once again the conscription of peasant labor). New systems of social control were required in areas of forced immigration, where there were no established blood relationships to ensure order. All of this led to the increased use of ruler-appointed professional administrators, who had jurisdiction over newly colonized or captured lands, or over specific governmental functions such as commanding troops; promoting agriculture; and creating population registers (like a census), tax records, crop statistics, maps, and law codes.

The state of Qin began this process early and continued to lead. It enjoyed strong leadership from several long-lived rulers, it was remarkably open to employing talented men from other states, and it faced little internal opposition. In addition, Qin had a geographical advantage that could not be matched by other kingdoms; it was located in a fertile, strategically situated region in west China, where protective mountain ranges made it a natural stronghold. The expanded agricultural production in Qin allowed it to put armies with tens of thousands of men in the field armed with crossbows (about one thousand years earlier than crossbows appeared in the West, with devastating results; see Figure 1) and reinforced by cavalry. In the end, due to a combination of skilled generals, talented administrators, natural resources, and perhaps a bit of luck, the consolidation of China by Qin was unstoppable. Qin armies overthrew the king of Zhou in 256 with hardly a complaint from states that had once based their own authority on their relationship to the Zhou. The state of Hann fell in 230, and the rest toppled in quick order: Zhao in 228, Wei in 225, Chu in 223, Yan in 222, and finally Qi in 221 (see Map 1).[4] The man who oversaw the final triumph of Qin was King Zheng (*Jung*; see Figure 2), who had come to the throne in 246 (at the age of thirteen). After conquering all of China, he established a new government and a new dynasty.

THE QIN DYNASTY (221–207 B.C.E.)

Having defeated all his rivals, King Zheng decided that a name change was in order. The prestige of the term "king" had diminished over the last century, and he needed something that would clearly demonstrate to the world that his power was both unprecedented and unchallengeable. After conferring with his advisers, he created the title "First August Emperor" (Shi Huangdi, *Sure Whahng-dee*) by combining two ancient terms that meant "sovereign" and "divinity." In doing so, he rejected the Zhou tradition of assigning royal names posthumously and decreed that he would forever be known as the "First Emperor," his son would be referred to as the "Second Emperor," his grandson as the "Third Emperor," and so on down to the ten-thousandth generation. He then implemented a whole series of symbolic changes intended to reinforce the idea that the Qin was a new dynasty that equaled or even surpassed the ancient Zhou regime. As mentioned above, many thinkers at the time believed that political change on earth mirrored the natural sequence of the Five Phases of Earth, Wood, Metal, Fire, and Water. Because theorists held that the Zhou dynasty had ruled by the power of Fire, and Fire could be

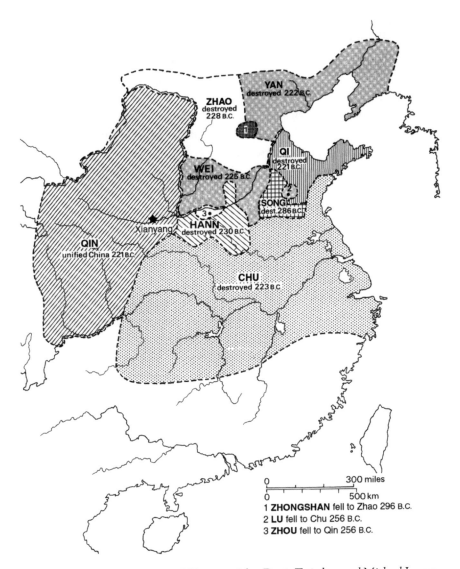

Map 1. Pre-imperial China, c. 250 B.C.E. *After Denis Twitchett and Michael Loewe, eds.,* The Cambridge History of China, *Vol. 1: The Ch'in and Han Empires 221 B.C.–A.D. 220 (New York: Cambridge University Press, 1986), p. 39. Reprinted with the permission of Cambridge University Press.*

conquered by Water, the First Emperor made Water the official phase of his new dynasty, along with its corresponding color (black) and auspicious number (six). Thus, court robes and flags were black, hats were six inches tall, and the imperial six-foot-wide carriage was drawn by six horses. He also ordered the carving of stone inscriptions on sacred mountains, which praised his rule and served as propaganda for the dynasty (see Figure 3 and Document 2).

Several ministers petitioned the First Emperor to follow the example of the Zhou dynasty and establish his relatives as subordinate kings who would rule over local territories on his behalf. However, the Commandant of Justice Li Si (*Lee Suh*) argued that it was precisely this feudal political structure that had weakened the previous dynasty, and he recommended instead that the emperor refashion all of China in the image of the state of Qin. This is what the First Emperor did, dividing China into thirty-six commanderies (six times six), each ruled by a governor, a military commander, and an imperial inspector, all three of whom were appointed by the central government. Each commandery in turn was subdivided into counties, and the emperor appointed and removed county magistrates at will. He introduced a new system of official ranks that organized the entire population in a hierarchy of some twenty levels. The First Emperor standardized weights and measures (see Figure 4), coinage, the axle-length of carts (to facilitate travel on roads with wheel ruts), and the writing system. In fact, the script mandated by the First Emperor was the basis for the writing system that is still in use in China today. He ordered a strict law code put in place (see Document 3) and commanded that weapons from all over the empire be collected and melted down to be recast as bells and statues. He even relocated 120,000 wealthy families of the old aristocracy to the capital where he could better control them. This massive reorganization was coordinated through regular, written reports, and the First Emperor, in good Legalist fashion, specified by weight the number of documents that he wanted to see every day (records were written on thin strips of bamboo bundled together; see Figures 5 and 6).

In addition, the First Emperor initiated a massive construction program of roads, walls, canals, palaces, and his own tomb, all built by conscripted labor. This last endeavor continues to impress people today, for it included the famous underground terra-cotta army that was discovered in the 1970s in the outskirts of the city of Xi'an, in Lintong near the ancient Qin capital Xianyang (*Sheyn yahng*). Over seven thousand individualized, life-size clay soldiers were created and arranged in battle formations within three large pits about a mile east of the First Emperor's tomb. The ghost army included infantry, cavalry, chariots, and an officer's command post, with all the soldiers brightly painted and armed with actual weapons. Then they were buried over, to be forgotten for more than two thousand years. Even in an age of skyscrapers and computers, the scale (and wastefulness) of this project is breathtaking. The actual tomb itself, which is reported to have included a scale model of China with flowing rivers of mercury and automatic crossbows guarding the entrance, has never been excavated.

Once the First Emperor had acquired such unprecedented power, he intended to enjoy it as long as he could, and a constant stream of would-be advisers came to court suggesting various policies. One Confucian again urged that feudalism should be restored, and again Li Si, now chancellor, argued forcefully for a strong central government. The emperor, angry that people were criticizing him by comparing him unfavorably to great kings of the past, responded by outlawing history. He ordered that all books in private hands be destroyed except for practical works on medicine, divination, and agriculture (this had been Li Si's advice), and he particularly targeted the Confucian classics (see Document 4). Later he made sure that scholars got the point by executing 460 of them. More to his liking were men who claimed to know magical secrets. One expert suggested that a ruler would gain spiritual power by assuming an aura of mystery, so that ordinary people never saw him or heard his voice. This made sense to the First Emperor, who had already survived three assassination attempts, and he began to live more secretively. He also began to take a keen interest in the elixir of immortality that had been promised by his magicians. When years passed without their being able to produce this miraculous drug, they made excuses that they could not get to the island where it was located because of a sea monster. The First Emperor, ever decisive, announced that he was going to the coast to kill this beast himself. He did manage to shoot an extraordinarily large fish with his automatic crossbow, but before his journey was completed, he died suddenly, in 210, at the age of forty-nine.

At this point Zhao Gao (*Jau Gau*), a senior eunuch (a castrated official in charge of household affairs for the royal family), approached Chancellor Li Si and informed him that the emperor was dead and that they were the only ones who knew it. He suggested that they pretend their ruler was still alive so that they could place on the throne someone they could control. They continued to send food into the imperial carriage and orders kept coming out, but these edicts were forged by the two ministers. A suicide order went to the heir apparent, Fusu (Foo sue), who thereupon killed himself, and then they arranged for the Emperor's not-so-bright son Huhai (Who hi) to be named as Second Emperor. Meanwhile, they rushed the imperial entourage back to the capital, the center of command. On the way, however, in the scorching summer heat, the stench of death started to emanate from the emperor's carriage, and the two plotters made sure a cart of salted fish was placed in the procession to cover the smell.

With the new emperor in power, things began to go wrong almost immediately. When the Second Emperor expressed concern that his officials and brothers might not obey him, Zhao Gao suggested that he apply the law even more harshly. "Excellent," he replied, and he thereupon executed high ministers and imperial princes. So many officials were accused of crimes and arrested that no one felt secure. The Second Emperor continued his father's massive building projects, and also enlarged the army and increased taxes. He even had the extravagant idea of lacquering the city walls. No one dared to speak out, but people everywhere were suffering. One of those caught short by such harsh measures was Chen She (Chun Shuh), a common laborer who, along with nine hundred other men from his native region, was assigned to guard the northern border several hundred miles away. The men set out for their destination, but as rains washed out the road, they got further and further behind schedule. Of course, the penalty for showing up late for guard duty was death. Finally the point came when Chen realized that they had nothing to lose—they would die if they continued on, and they would die if they deserted. So, following his advice, the conscripts killed their officers and became rebels (see Document 5). In fact, all over China men revolted—attacking Qin officials, raising armies, seizing territory, and declaring themselves kings.

When a messenger came to the court to report Chen She's uprising, the Second Emperor was furious and had the messenger arrested. Not surprisingly, messengers quit bringing bad news, though the dynasty itself was endangered. Even Li Si was executed when he dared to inform the emperor that he was losing power. When the imperial troops could no longer keep order, Zhao Gao forced the Second Emperor to commit suicide, and then attempted to claim the empire for himself. No one would follow or obey him, so he set up a nephew of the Second Emperor as king of Qin (the title emperor no longer made sense). This unfortunate ruler is remembered for only two actions—he killed Zhao Gao in a surprise attack, and then, after only forty-six days on the throne, he surrendered the capital in 206 to one of the major rebels, Liu Bang, the man who four years later would found the Han dynasty. In retrospect, it appears that the Qin dynasty tried to change too much too fast, and there was too much power concentrated at the top of the government. So instead of the "ten thousand years" envisioned by the First Emperor, the dynasty lasted only four years after his death, making fourteen years in all. (For an early Han assessment of the Qin Empire, see Document 9.)

CIVIL WAR (209–202 B.C.E.)

The fighting started with Chen She's rebellion in 209, just after the Second Emperor had taken power. As the historian Sima Qian later told the story, "Chen She was made king and he took the title 'Expander of Chu.' At this time, in every commandery and county, those who had suffered under Qin officials took revenge on the magistrates and officials and murdered them in order to ally themselves with Chen She."[5] Chen She himself lasted only six months as king before he was assassinated by his chariot driver—who claimed loyalty to the Qin—but Chen set in motion a series of rebellions that would overwhelm the dynasty. It is striking that Chen claimed to be restoring the old kingdom of Chu. The feudal states had been gone for only a few decades, and they made a convenient rallying point for ambitious soldiers, conservative scholars, ex-aristocrats, and peasants who had known only sorrow under the Qin.

Chen She's desire to return to the feudal system also held out the implicit promise of territory in return for military service. In other words, it seemed that there were opportunities for capable individuals to join the ranks of the aristocracy and then pass on lands and privileges to their own children. Not surprisingly, when Chen sent one of his generals to capture the region of Zhao (*Jau*), this man quickly (and without authorization) declared himself the king of Zhao. Since Chen She did not have enough troops to forcibly set him straight, he grudgingly acknowledged the claim. Similarly, when the new king of Zhao sent one of his commanders to Yan (*Yen*), that former state soon gained a new, self-proclaimed king. Two other rebels grabbed the titles of king in Qi and Wei. These men kept one eye on the Qin imperial troops who were sent to quash them, and another eye on each other. If they had had a third eye, they could have used it to watch out for their subordinates, who themselves were willing to double-cross and assassinate in their scramble for power.

It was a dangerous time, and when the Qin dynasty collapsed, the conflict between rebel leaders only intensified. Each tried to size up his competitors and ally himself with the one who seemed to have the most potential for success. In doing so, they were well aware that they were gambling with both their own lives and those of their men. They were keen to observe signs that they were resented or mistrusted by their allies, or that it might be a good time to switch sides, or that taking a large risk might result in a significant advantage, or that arriving late for a battle might let them avoid a disastrous loss. Many would not live to see the establishment of the next dynasty. Though they all hoped that China would be unified once again, it was unclear who would gain control of the country, much less claim the Mandate of Heaven.

In time, the rebel armies came together around two leaders—Xiang Yu and Liu Bang (later known by his imperial title Gaozu [*Gau-zoo*; "Exalted Ancestor"]; see Figures 7 and 8). Xiang Yu, unusually tall and strong, was a descendent of a noble family in the state of Chu (*Choo*). He was arrogant, impetuous, and impatient with details, but he was easily the most capable military commander of the time. Liu Bang, on the other hand, started life as a peasant in Chu and was eventually appointed village head. He was easygoing and fond of wine, but through a canny combination of kindness and ruthlessness, he inspired astounding loyalty in his followers. He also knew when to take advice and when to reverse course.

In their early years, both Xiang Yu and Liu Bang had caught a glimpse of the First Emperor, and both were envious, though it is telling how each responded. Xiang declared, "That guy could be taken and replaced." Liu, more wistfully, sighed and exclaimed, "Ah, that is how it should be for a great man." So, also, they rebelled in very different ways. Xiang treacherously assassinated a governor and quickly recruited eight thousand men to attack the Qin. Liu, as a village head, was assigned to escort prisoners to work on the First Emperor's tomb. When so many escaped that he feared for his life, he got drunk, let the rest go, and became an outlaw himself. His first followers were a dozen of his former prisoners who asked if they could stay with him. In the contest between the aristocratic, driven commander and the casual, dreamy peasant, only one man could win.

Xiang Yu gradually distinguished himself as the only general who could regularly defeat imperial troops. He had the largest, most powerful army, and the other rebel leaders were forced to work closely with him. For instance, they had all agreed that whoever captured the Qin capital could thereafter rule that strategically positioned territory. When Liu Bang's troops moved in first and accepted the surrender of the king of Qin (this was the nephew of the Second Emperor, in the sixth week of his reign), Liu tried to block the passes and keep other rebels out (see Document 6). Xiang Yu, who suddenly had grave misgivings about the agreement, was furious that he had been bested and showed up with four hundred thousand soldiers. Since Liu only commanded one hundred thousand men, he judiciously stepped aside and claimed that he had simply been guarding the capital region until he could hand it over to Xiang Yu. Xiang summoned Liu to a formal meeting, but it soon became obvious that Xiang's advisors were goading their boss into executing Liu. Xiang hesitated and Liu narrowly escaped when he pretended he had to relieve himself and then slipped out the back.

By 206, the year after the fall of the Qin dynasty, it looked like Xiang Yu would be the next ruler of China. His plan was to restore the old feudal system with kings in various regions administering their territories under the guidance of one powerful, dominant kingdom, and it seemed obvious to him that his native kingdom of Chu should take that leading role. Early in the war he had located the grandson of the last king of Chu in a field where he was tending sheep, and had elevated him to the position of king. Eventually, however, realizing that royal blood was not as significant as military power, he conferred the honorary title "Righteous Emperor" on the man, only to have him assassinated a few months later. In any case, Xiang Yu was the one who decided which rebel generals would become king over which territories. He kept Chu for himself and then, as "hegemon-king" (or "leading king"), he set up eighteen other deputy kings. Liu Bang did not get the Qin heartland he had expected, but was instead made the king of Han, the region just south of Qin.[6] After asserting his authority and dividing up China, Xiang Yu marched east with his troops back to Chu.

He never made it there, for almost immediately the new kings started attacking each other, and Xiang Yu had to move quickly to enforce his orders. Liu Bang, claiming that he had been cheated out of territory that was rightfully his and criticizing Xiang Yu for murdering the Righteous Emperor, took the region of Qin from the three kings whom Xiang had appointed there. For the next four years, Xiang Yu and Liu Bang fought each other, while the other kings allied themselves first with one and then the other, depending on who looked stronger. Often things did not go well for Liu, and twice he was surrounded by the forces of Xiang Yu only to stage a miraculous escape—once he was saved by a freak storm, and another time he fled when one of his soldiers agreed to serve as his disguised substitute. No matter how many battles Xiang Yu won, Liu Bang always seemed to elude his grasp, and just when Xiang was about to crush Liu's forces, attacks in other regions forced Xiang to take his men elsewhere.

Liu Bang enjoyed the geographic advantage of a base in the former state of Qin, even though one of Xiang Yu's men had warned Xiang not to give up the region:

> Someone advised King Xiang, "The area within the passes is blocked by mountains and rivers which form a barrier on all sides, and the territory is fertile; so it is a suitable place in which to establish a capital city in order to rule as hegemon-king." But King Xiang saw that the palaces of Qin had all been destroyed by fire [ironically, at the hands of his own troops], and he also cherished in his heart the desire to return home east. "If riches and honors are not taken back to one's place of origin," he said, "it is like going out at night wearing embroideries, for who is there who will know about it?" The person who gave the advice said: "People say that the men of Chu are only monkeys with caps on, and it's quite true." When King Xiang heard this, he had the man who gave the advice immersed in boiling water.[7]

Xiang Yu's cruel reaction to good advice was not atypical, and in this case his miscalculation about where to locate his capital proved crucial.

At another time, Xiang Yu captured Liu Bang's father and threatened to boil him alive if Liu refused to surrender. Liu sent back a message reminding Xiang Yu that they had once sworn to be brothers. He continued, "Therefore my father is your father, too. If you insist now upon boiling your own father, I hope you will be good enough to send me a cup of the soup!"[8] Xiang Yu was furious and wanted to kill Liu's father, but an advisor persuaded him that he would do well to show a higher morality than Liu Bang, so he let the old man go. In the end, however, it did him little good. Xiang Yu was kind at the wrong moments, and harsh when it was not advantageous.

In 203, when the two armies were at a stalemate, Xiang Yu challenged Liu to fight him in one-to-one combat, with the winner taking all of China. Liu refused with a laugh, saying, "Since I can't compete with you in strength, I prefer to fight with brains." Xiang, enraged, pulled out a crossbow and shot Liu, but the wound was not fatal, and a few months later the two agreed to divide China between them. Xiang Yu, with his exhausted, poorly supplied soldiers, once again headed east toward Chu, and Liu, once again, double-crossed him by immediately launching an attack on his rear (with the help of two generals whom he had just made kings).

This time it was Xiang Yu who was surrounded, and when he could hear the songs of Chu from the opposing camp (indicating how many of the men from his native region were now with Liu Bang), he knew that the end had come. After an eight-year campaign and over the course of seventy battles—nearly all of which he had won—Xiang Yu said good-bye to his horse and his mistress, then fought three more quick skirmishes in which he killed several dozen men and sustained wounds in ten places. Finally, as Liu's troops closed in, he cut his own throat. The soldiers tore his body to pieces in their eagerness to grab his corpse so that they could claim the reward for bringing in his head.

Liu Bang, who had been appointed king of Han four years earlier, was now in the same position that Xiang Yu had been in. It seemed that he had bested his rivals, but with tens of thousands of armed men still in the field and ambitious generals planning their next moves, it might all fall apart. That was when his advisers asked him to declare himself emperor (not just "hegemon-king") and establish a new dynasty—the Han—named after his first kingdom. And that is just what he did, at the coronation ceremony of February 202 (see Document 8).

THE HAN DYNASTY (202 B.C.E.–220 C.E.)

Liu's first task was to reward his followers in the hopes of keeping their loyalty. Like Xiang Yu, he handed out kingdoms, fiefs, and noble ranks right and left. Some of the former kings who had allied themselves with Liu kept their positions, others were transferred, and some key generals became new kings. Liu ordered the armies disbanded, freed those who had been enslaved during the conflict, and proclaimed a reduction in taxes. Nevertheless, some of his old generals were still restive, and Liu had to lead troops to quell two rebellions before the end of his first year as emperor. Liu kept fighting for the rest of his life, and before his death in 195 he had to deal with five more revolts and an assassination attempt, as well as lead a campaign against the Xiongnu (Shee-ong new), the nomadic horsemen in the north whose raids had led the First Emperor to build a fortified precursor to the Great Wall. When Liu was nearly captured in that expedition, he agreed to a peace treaty under which the Xiongnu promised not to invade China in return for gifts of silk, rice, wine, and a Chinese princess. All this fighting caught up with Liu in the end, for he died from an illness made worse by an infected arrow wound.

Yet oddly enough, political stability would come from this inauspicious beginning and Liu's descendants would rule China for the next four hundred years. How did this happen? Perhaps, as some Han scholars suggested, it was simply the Mandate of Heaven, a matter of destiny. For modern historians, however, three major reasons come to mind. The first was Liu's exceptional skill in managing men, the second was the basic structure of the government he established, and the third was the Han Empire's adoption of Confucianism as an official ideology. With regard to the first explanation, Liu was able to both recognize unusual talent and keep these individuals as his allies. Both aspects were mentioned at a grand banquet that Liu held for his followers shortly after he became emperor, when he asked the critical question himself:

> "My lords and generals, I ask you all to speak your minds quite frankly without daring to hide anything from me. Why is it that I won possession of the world and Xiang Yu lost?"
>
> Gao Qi and Wang Ling replied, "Your Majesty is arrogant and insulting to others, while Xiang Yu was kind and loving. But when you send someone to attack a city or seize a region, you award him the spoils of the victory, sharing your gains with the whole world. Xiang Yu was jealous of worth and ability, hating those who had achieved merit and suspecting anyone who displayed his wisdom. No matter what victories were achieved in battle, he gave his men no reward;

no matter what lands they won, he never shared with them the spoils. This is why he lost possession of the world."

Liu Bang said, "You have understood the first reason, but you do not know the second. When it comes to sitting within the tents of command and devising strategies that will assure us victory a thousand miles away, I am no match for Zhang Liang. In ordering the state and caring for the people, in providing rations for the troops and seeing to it that the lines of supply are not cut off, I cannot compare to Xiao He. In leading an army of a million men, achieving success with every battle and victory with every attack, I cannot come up to Han Xin. These three are all men of extraordinary ability, and it is because I was able to make use of them that I gained possession of the world. Xiang Yu had his one Fan Zeng, but he did not know how to use him and thus he ended as my prisoner."[9]

Liu's relationship with each of his three main advisers demonstrates his skill in assessing and utilizing men. Zhang Liang (*Johng Lee-ong*) was a run-of-the-mill bandit chief with a band of one hundred men when he first met Liu Bang. The future emperor, however, recognizing his spirit (he had once tried to assassinate the First Emperor) and his tactical abilities (he claimed to have a secret book of military strategy), put his full trust in him despite the fact that he did not have a tough, soldierly appearance. Time and again Zhang gave him exactly the right advice. Xiao He (*Shau Huh*) was a Qin official in the region where Liu grew up. He had helped Liu in his duties as village head, and then joined Liu Bang when he rebelled. Later, Xiao was put in charge of recruiting soldiers and sending supplies, and when Liu had first captured the Qin capital, Xiao He had wisely seized the maps, population registries, and other records of the Qin government. Xiao was such a capable administrator that Liu rewarded him more lavishly than even his generals by giving him the post of prime minister. Han Xin (*Hahn Sheen*) was a nobody—someone who had once narrowly escaped execution and who had just run away from service—when Liu Bang brought him back and, in a grand ceremony, made him a major general. From a management perspective, it was an extraordinarily risky promotion. In retrospect, it was a brilliant move; Han Xin's abilities as a general were astonishing (see Document 7). Liu could not have done anything without the talents of these three men, and he knew it.

The second factor in the success of the dynasty was the basic government system that Liu put in place. Following the model of the Qin, the new government standardized laws, assessed taxes (in both grain and labor service), and established twenty ranks of nobility, with advancement based on merit. Liu also wisely balanced the need to reward his followers with feudal estates against the efficiency of the new style of bureaucratic administration perfected by the Qin dynasty. The eastern two-thirds of the empire was divided into ten kingdoms, while the western third was organized into fourteen commanderies that were directly overseen by the central government (see Map 2). The new kings gave Liu immediate assistance in collecting taxes, administering justice, and defending borders, but as the various kings revolted, Liu replaced them with his own brothers and sons, so that by the time of his death, all but one of these kingdoms were ruled by members of the Liu family. In addition to the kingdoms, there were some one hundred and fifty marquises who were entitled to tax revenues from territories of various sizes, and this highest rank was the only one that could be passed on to one's descendants.

The central government was divided into three branches—the military, the civil service, and the censorate (whose job was to spy on other officials and report to the emperor). In the United States, we also have three branches of government, a system designed to protect the rights of citizens by ensuring that no one person gains enough power to become a dictator. In China, the government was divided in order to protect the emperor. By separating the men with weapons from the men who collected taxes—and spying on both—the emperor could prevent any one man or group of men from monopolizing enough resources to challenge his authority. The pattern was repeated at the local level, where each commandery and each county was governed by a combination of a military commander and a civilian authority. A little later, regional inspectors were also appointed to report directly to the emperor on how these officials were carrying out their duties.

County magistrates had enormous power since they were responsible for functions that today we would categorize as judicial, legislative, and executive. They supervised the collection of taxes, the maintenance of waterways, the formulation of policy, the arresting and sentencing of criminals, the conscription of men for military service and labor projects, the promotion of agriculture, the settling of disputes, the registration and counting of the population, the suppression of rebellion, and the re-

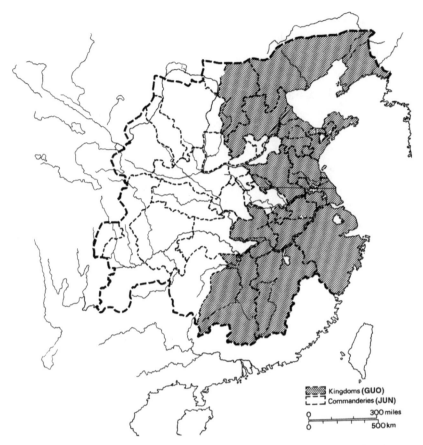

Map 2. The Han Empire, 163 B.C.E. *After Denis Twitchett and Michael Loewe, eds.*, The Cambridge History of China, Vol. 1: The Ch'in and Han Empires 221 B.C.–A.D. 220 *(New York: Cambridge University Press, 1986), p. 138. Reprinted with the permission of Cambridge University Press.*

cruitment of new officials. Such wide-ranging authority needed to be controlled in some way, and the central government required regular reports from magistrates, in addition to tying salaries and promotion to performance, and instituting the "rule of avoidance," which meant that no one was allowed to serve in his native district (to prevent nepotism and corruption). In time, however, the state discovered the most useful tool in motivating officials and keeping them honest—Confucianism—the third reason that the Han dynasty prospered.

Before he came to power, Liu Bang—uneducated and inclined toward military matters—had little use for Confucian scholars who were always talking about their books, ancient ceremonies, and theories of ethics. In fact, when Liu met a Confucian scholar wearing his robes and distinctive cap, he would grab the hat from the surprised man's head and urinate into it to show his disdain. But everything changed when he became emperor. Once, when he cursed an ambassador who praised the Confucian classics, the official cautioned him that the skills needed to conquer an empire were quite different from those needed to govern it ("You may have won the world on horseback, but can you rule it on horseback?").[10] And the advantages of Confucian ideals of order, hierarchy, and humane concern soon became obvious. Shusun Tong (*Shoe-swun Toeng*), a Confucian scholar, arranged the titles and ritual used at the coronation in 202. After the armies were sent home, when some of Liu's military men hung around the palace arguing, getting drunk, and hacking at the pillars with their swords, Shusun stepped forward and volunteered to set up an appropriate protocol for the court. "Confucians are hard to use when marching forward to conquer," he said, "but they are good allies in holding on to what one has gained."[11] Liu's first concern was that the court etiquette not be too hard to learn, but he soon appreciated the increased respect that came from rules and ritual.

Liu had already shown tendencies toward Confucian concern for the common people, even if he had not formally studied that tradition. When he first captured the area of the Qin capital, he spared the life of the surrendering last ruler of Qin, prevented his soldiers from looting, and published the following proclamation:

> You elders have long suffered under Qin's harsh laws. Those who criticized the government were exterminated with their three kindred. Those who gathered to discuss the *Songs* and the *Documents* were executed and had their bodies exposed in the marketplace. I should be the king of the Land within the Passes, since I have agreed with the feudal lords that whoever enters the Pass first should rule over it as king. I will come to an agreement with you elders that there will be a legal code with only three articles: those who kill a person must die, those who injure a person and steal will be punished according to the offense. I will do away with all the rest of Qin's laws. All the officers and people will live in peace as before. Do not be afraid—I have come to do away with that which causes you elders harm, not to impose tyranny![12]

Confucius would have been proud. (Xiang Yu, by contrast, killed the ex-ruler of Qin, massacred the populace, and burned the city when he took over the capital.) When Liu managed to win the entire empire four years later, he implemented the principles outlined above and deliberately ruled in a more benevolent manner than either the First Emperor or Xiang Yu. Yet the Han dynasty he founded was in some ways built on a lie, for it is impossible to govern an empire with a three-article law code. What actually happened was that the Han kept most of the institutional framework of the Qin—its laws, governmental organization, and administrative practices—yet it applied those political methods in the humane manner usually associated with Confucianism. This, then, was the secret to the astonishing success of the Chinese imperial system—it combined the centralization and coercion of Legalism with the kinder, more flexible ideology of Confucianism. Still, it is important to note that Confucianism was not elevated as the state creed until the reign of Emperor Wu, and even then, it was one among many ideologies that influenced the court. It was not until the end of the Former Han that imperial policy began to be consciously dominated by Confucian ideas. Nevertheless, Liu Bang's efforts represent a first step toward Confucianizing the state.

There were important refinements in statecraft over the next hundred years. Liu's widow tried to shift important offices to her own family, only to have the principle of Liu family domination reaffirmed when her brothers and other relatives were executed after her death in 180. The next two rulers, Emperors Wen (*One*; r. 180–157) and Jing (*Jeeng*; r. 157–141), were respectively the son and grandson of Liu Bang, and together they ruled for almost forty years. Their reigns were remembered as times of relative peace and prosperity, as China recovered from decades of civil war and political conflict. The reach of the central government was gradually extended as kingdoms were replaced by commanderies (especially after seven kingdoms revolted in 154), and Emperor Jing began to divest the kings of their authority by appointing the senior officials in the remaining kingdoms. The territories controlled by marquises were confiscated by the state when rulers died without heirs or were accused of crimes. Under the remarkable fifty-four-year reign of Emperor Wu (*Woo*; r. 141–87), the power of the central government was strengthened as he aggressively attacked the northern barbarians, expanded the empire, regulated the economy—by creating state monopolies for salt, iron, and alcohol—and moved decisively against the remaining kingdoms and hereditary marquisates. At the same time, he promoted Confucianism by sponsoring Erudite (or learned) Scholars of the Confucian Classics, founding the Imperial Academy, and recruiting officials systematically (thus paving the way for the famous civil-service exams in later dynasties). And finally, during the reign of Emperor Wu, the grand historian Sima Qian wrote the first history of imperial China, a work that provided the material for nearly all of this chapter.

But the ultimate credit belongs to Liu Bang. After assuming the title of emperor in 202 and founding the Han dynasty, he set on its course one of the most effective institutions in the history of the world—imperial China. The imperial system, with its emphasis on scholar-bureaucrats, lasted for another two thousand years in China, and even today the ideal of government by officials qualified by merit rather than birth is with us, as is the attraction of a strong legal system tempered by humane concerns. China continues into the present as a large, powerful, unified country, and it is fitting that its people still refer to themselves as *Han ren* (*Hahn run*), "the people of Han."

NOTES

1. Unless otherwise noted, all dates in this book are B.C.E. (before the common era)—a designation equivalent to the more familiar B.C. The abbreviation C.E. is short for "common era," which is a religiously neutral equivalent of A.D.

2. *Shiji*, 8.379; see Burton Watson, trans., *Records of the Grand Historian, Han Dynasty*, 2 vols., rev. ed. (New York and Hong Kong: *Renditions*-Columbia University Press, 1993), 1:75.

3. In Chinese, Confucius is referred to as *Kongzi*, or "Master Kong" ("Confucius" is a Latinized form introduced by Jesuit missionaries), and his school was called Ruism. The word *ru* meant something like "soft or weak" and referred to scholars and officials who had no military responsibilities. Confucius became the foremost teacher in this school, and he and his students gathered together the classic texts of ancient China and became experts in their transmission and interpretation. There were, however, other scholars of classical texts who claimed the title of *ru* but were not followers of Confucius. In general, the philosophical schools of early China were not well-defined until the Han dynasty.

4. The region of Hann is quite distinct from the Han of the Han dynasty. The two names are represented in Chinese by entirely different characters, but because they sound similar, it is customary to spell the first place-name with a double *n*.

5. *Shiji*, 48.1953; see Watson, *Han*, 1:4.

6. The Han dynasty is often reckoned to have begun in 206, when Liu Bang was named the king of Han, but he did not gain control of all of China until 202.

7. Dawson's translation, in *Sima Qian: Historical Records*, translated by Raymond Dawson (Oxford: Oxford University Press, 1994), p. 126 (mod.).

8. Watson's translation, *Han*, 1:41.

9. Watson's translation, *Han*, 1:76.

10. *Shiji*, 97.2699; see Watson, *Han*, 1:226.

11. *Shiji*, 99.2722; see Watson, *Han*, 1:242.

12. Nienhauser's translation, in William H. Nienhauser, Jr., et al., trans., *The Grand Scribe's Records* (Bloomington: Indiana University Press, 2002), 2:38–39.

CHAPTER 2

THE CENTER AND THE PERIPHERY

Traditional Chinese historiography presents the transition from the Shang dynasty (c. 1570–1045 B.C.E.) to the Zhou dynasty (1045–256 B.C.E.) as a smooth process. It was simply a matter of one clan losing and another receiving the Mandate of Heaven and the territory of "all under Heaven" that went with it. From the perspective of modern archaeology, the story is much more complicated. At the time the Zhou gained control of North China, half a dozen early Bronze Age (1500–1000 B.C.E.) societies inhabited the area, each with a distinctive artistic style and presumably different religions and customs as well. The Zhou kings adopted the Shang kings at Anyang as their predecessors, but the idea of political unity in China was a myth that the Zhou created in an attempt to bolster their own claim to power.

In addition to the semi-independent territories that the first Zhou kings had bestowed as fiefs to their royal relatives, over the course of the dynasty, Zhou rulers expanded their borders and populace by bringing more regions into their political system and cultural domain. In theory, "barbarian" tribes pledged allegiance to the Zhou royal house and in return received a confirmation of their territorial claims. In practice, it meant that a walled city was established by a local clan with military, religious, and cultural ties to the Zhou kings. By the Spring and Autumn Era (722–481), peoples once thought of as barbarians had established large and powerful states in border regions. These included Qin in the west, Chu in the south along the Yangzi River, and Wu and Yue on the coast just south of where the Yangzi runs into the China Sea. Yet there were nomadic tribes beyond these newly civilized states, and indeed the *Spring and Autumn Annals* mentions peoples within the Chinese heartland who were still independent, living in the rural areas between the Zhou-affiliated cities. These included the Man people in the south, the Yi in the east, the Rong in the west, and the Di in the north.

Once local rulers began to organize their states by territory rather than by feudal ties, the Zhou-affiliated kingdoms gained greater control over their regions and eventually became more powerful than the state of Zhou itself. Whereas responsibilities and privileges used to be based on aristocratic rank, rulers now sought to unify their kingdoms by bestowing rank as a reward for merit and imposing more universal standards of taxation and military service on their populace. In 594 the state of Lu (Confucius' native state) began to assess taxes according to the acreage held by each family. Four years later it introduced universal military conscription, following the lead of the state of Jin. Under this new system, all men within a given territory, regardless of ethnic background, were fighting side by side in the same army. The state of Chu was apparently the first to organize newly conquered lands into *xian* (*shyen*)—that is, small administrative divisions governed not by a hereditary feudal lord but by an official appointed by the ruler of the state. In 548, in a policy designed to control and utilize the people and lands within its borders more effectively, Chu began to register its population for military and taxation purposes. In 513 the state of Jin wrote its laws on a bronze vessel. Other states followed each innovation in centralization, with the state of Qin becoming spectacularly successful in its consolidation of central authority and corresponding weakening of aristocratic power at the local level.

And thus the balance of power shifted. As states on the periphery became more organized and more powerful, the central political position held by the Zhou kings declined. Zhou culture, including writings and rituals, was still predominant, with a wider reach than ever before, but the house of Zhou could no longer dictate what was happening beyond its borders. By 256 it no longer controlled even its own territory. The Zhou kingdom was taken over by Qin in that year, and despite the rapid centralization taking place within competing states, Qin conquered them one by one until it finally united all of China within a single empire.

Both the Qin and the Han empires faced a similar challenge. Governing a large territory requires the assistance of authorities in far-flung regions. By necessity, rulers had to allot considerable military and financial resources to such men so that they could perform their administrative functions. But once these allies were firmly in control of their local area, what was to prevent them from employing their resources against the central government? Such challenges could come gradually, as local administrators worked to increase their power and autonomy, or they could take the form of full-scale rebellions. In either case, central authorities had to expend enormous effort to keep control of the periphery, both to preserve their borders intact and to ensure their own survival. The Qin emperors failed at this task, while the Han succeeded, but just barely.

THE STRUCTURE OF GOVERNMENT

Power in the Qin and Han empires can be represented by the diagram on p. 32 (the specific details changed over time, but this at least will provide a general idea). At the top, of course, was the emperor. He was a man of immense power and authority, who could hand out rewards and punishments at will, even executing those who displeased him. Yet he could not govern by himself. The emperor needed a military with capable commanders to expand his territories and keep out the nomadic tribes. He needed civil administrators (the outer court) to collect taxes, organize construction projects, and keep order. He needed the servants and family members of the inner court to care for his personal needs. But most of all he needed the loyalty of all of these people. When the emperor was able to effectively employ talented individuals, balancing them against each other and preventing any one person or group from becoming powerful enough to overthrow him, then he was successful. It took nearly a century and a half from the initial conquest of China by the First Emperor in 221 to firmly establish the imperial system that would institutionalize these checks and balances.

The division of the government into three branches dated back to the Qin Empire. The senior official of the civil branch was the chancellor (though at times there were two co-chancellors, called chancellors of the left and right). As the head of the outer court he was the most powerful man in the administration, working directly with the emperor to evaluate reports and set policy, though he was never next in line to the throne (that position was held by the heir apparent). The chancellor was slightly superior to his two colleagues in the other branches of government—the supreme commander, who oversaw the military, and the imperial coun-

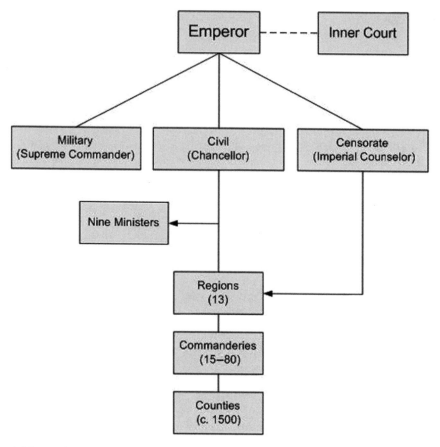

Additional concerns outside the central government included kingdoms (10–30), non-Chinese peoples, and merchants.

selor, who provided an auditing function and reported directly to the emperor on the behavior of other government officials (I have used the later term "censorate" to describe this third branch).

Under the chancellor were nine ministers, each of whom headed a government bureau. These included the departments of ceremony, the palace, trials, palace guards, transport, state visits, the imperial clan, agriculture, and the lesser treasury. Of these, the ministers of agriculture and the lesser treasury were charged with the collection of taxes. The entire Qin Empire was divided into commanderies—thirty-six in the beginning, then increasing to forty—and each was headed by three officials representing the military, the civil, and the censorate. At the beginning of the

Han, one-third of the empire was organized into fifteen commanderies while the rest of the land was divided among ten kings (see Map 2). However, because these kings posed a threat to dynastic stability, emperors actively decreased the size and independent power of the kingdoms and created new commanderies until there were eighty or so. Each Han commandery was subdivided into counties (eventually there were some fifteen hundred of these) and was headed by a civil governor and a military commandant. In 106 the empire was divided into thirteen regions, each of which included both commanderies and kingdoms, and thirteen regional inspectors were appointed. These men, however, were auditors rather than supervisors, and they were expected to report cases of injustice, corruption, or inefficiency. But the real power was still held by the commandery governors.

The inner court (connected to the emperor by a dotted line to indicate informal influence) consisted of the emperor's consorts and favorites, along with their family members. The inner court also included eunuchs who, because of their physical condition, were deemed trustworthy enough to be in the women's apartments. Eunuchs were also valued because they could not have families of their own and so would never be tempted to betray the emperor in order to advance their private interests—or at least that was the theory. The women and servants all had official positions in the civil service and received salaries based on these positions, though they were not supposed to meddle in governmental affairs. But even so, the empress dowager, for example, came to occupy an official function in confirming a new emperor.

INNER COURT PROBLEMS

As we saw in the last chapter, the Qin Empire was secure only as long as the First Emperor was directly controlling the government. It took only a few hours after his death for the eunuch Zhao Gao, a member of the inner court, to take advantage of his privileged access and begin plotting with the chancellor to change the heir apparent. Imperial succession was something that the emperor's wives (and their families) cared deeply about, and although the power of eunuchs did not surface again until the end of the Han Empire, in the early decades the question of succession almost brought the dynasty to a quick halt after the death of its founder Liu Bang. Liu had a principal wife named Empress Lü (*Lyoo*) and, like most emperors, numerous consorts as well. The empress had been married to him since he was a commoner and had borne him two children—a boy and a girl. Naturally, she wanted her son to become the next emperor.

Liu, however, had seven other sons by at least four other women, and he took a particular liking to Ruyi (*Rooyee*), the son of Lady Qi (*Chee*). Lady Qi begged Liu to make her own son the heir apparent, though her pleas were strenuously opposed by both Empress Lü and several senior members of the government, who were wary of the chaos that might result. The change was never made, but as soon as Liu Bang died, Empress Lü took her revenge. Although the real heir apparent, now Emperor Hui (*Whey*), took pity on his vulnerable, younger half-brother Ruyi and tried to protect him, Empress Lü succeeded in poisoning him. She also had his mother Lady Qi blinded, mutilated, and thrown into a privy. Emperor Hui never quite recovered from the shock of his mother's viciousness and died at the age of twenty-three after only seven years on the throne.

The power of Empress Lü only increased as she ruled as regent for two of her underage grandsons (both supposedly were sons of Emperor Hui, though their paternity was doubted even at the time), and she worked to secure the position of her own family by appointing three of her relatives as kings and several more as generals. There had once been an agreement that any new kings should come from the Liu family, and when Empress Lü died, some members of the imperial clan wanted to remove the Lü family from their kingdoms and offices. The Lü clan in turn began to plot to take over the empire and overthrow the dynasty. With the support of a key general and the chancellor, the Liu family gained the upper hand and all members of the Lü family were arrested and beheaded.

An empire needs an emperor, however, and there were three descendents of Liu Bang, all currently kings, who were candidates—two were his sons and another a grandson. The officials who had been crucial to preserving the rule of the Liu clan decided that the next emperor should be the one with the mother judged least likely to have political ambitions for herself and her family. And so it was that Liu Heng, the king of Dai, became Emperor Wen. The administrators seem to have chosen wisely, for the plotting of consort families did not pose a threat for the next couple of emperors. The kings, however, with their ability to amass taxes and troops, were an obvious challenge.

KINGDOM PROBLEMS

The Qin Empire eradicated the old kingdoms of the Warring States Era, and then discovered too late that those regional regimes continued to attract support more than a decade and a half after China's unification. Liu Bang and Xiang Yu, along with other military leaders, rallied their troops on behalf of pre-Qin kingdoms, and though Liu Bang would have probably preferred to rule China directly, he did not have the power to do so. Liu needed representatives who could collect taxes and keep order in far-off regions, but he had not yet established a bureaucracy—officials who served a ruler for a salary, and could be appointed or replaced at will. Moreover, those who had gained territory by force of arms would support the empire only if they could continue to control these lands and pass them on to their heirs. Liu inspired trust in his subordinates, but not that much.

This was clearly the case on the eve of Xiang Yu's destruction when Liu sent out one last call for his generals Han Xin (*Hahn Sheen*) and Peng Yue (*Pung You-eh*) to bring their troops to the battle. Neither showed up and Liu was soundly defeated. At that point he asked his main strategist Zhang Liang (*Johng Lee-ong*) what he should do. "The Chu army is on the point of being destroyed, Zhang Liang replied, but Han Xin and Peng Yue have not yet been granted any territory. It is not surprising that they do not come when summoned. If you will consent to share a part of the empire with them, they will surely come without a moment's hesitation."[1] Liu Bang agreed to make them both kings, and together the three armies brought an end to Xiang Yu.

When he finally became emperor in 202, Liu Bang was forced to compromise. In the western third of the empire, he divided the land into fifteen commanderies administered by salaried officials whom he appointed directly.[2] But to ensure the continuing support of his former generals and provide for the stability of border regions, he established ten hereditary kingdoms composed of the remaining two-thirds of the empire in the east. Among these new kings were Han Xin and Peng Yue, as promised. In general, the kings were men who had just recently come to prominence. People who claimed descent from the royal families of the pre-Qin kingdoms—the same social class from which the "Righteous Emperor" had come—survived, but Liu moved one hundred thousand of these remnants of the old aristocracy to the capital, where they would be under his close observation and cut off from their native lands. They never posed a challenge to his power.

The kings were required to report annually to the emperor in person, they had to turn over some of the taxes they collected, and they were not allowed to call out troops without explicit permission, but otherwise they were free to govern their territories as they saw fit. Problems arose almost immediately, however. Within six months, the king of Yan revolted. Liu Bang strapped on his armor and led his troops to the fight. In 200 the king of Hann joined with the Xiongnu (*Shee-ong new*) nomads and rebelled. Liu Bang rode into battle again, and though ultimately victorious, he was surrounded for seven days and nearly captured. In 196 Chen Xi, the prime minister of the kingdom of Dai, revolted, as did Han Xin, Peng Yue, and Qing Bu, one right after another (it was pretty clear that Liu did not trust the kings, and as a result they felt impelled to move before he did). As he dealt with rebellious kings, Liu replaced them with his own brothers and sons, so that the kingdoms looked quite different in 195 than they had seven years earlier. All the kings except one were Liu family members, and that exception was replaced by a Liu in 157. Yet the kingdoms were large and prosperous, and even relatives might be tempted to make a break for independence.

Emperors Wen (180–157) and Jing (157–141) heeded the advice of ministers who told them that the power of the kingdoms needed to be reduced, and they patiently did so. In 179, after the family of Empress Lü had been deposed, there were twenty commanderies and eleven kingdoms; by 143 there were forty-one commanderies and twenty-five kingdoms. Although the number of kingdoms had increased, they were much smaller and less independent, especially after 145 when the central government asserted the right to appoint each king's senior ministers. Along with fulfilling their administrative duties, these men also reported to the emperor on the behavior of the kings, and eventually the differences between the commanderies and the kingdoms became less significant.

Much of this change occurred slowly, as portions of kingdoms were reassigned to commanderies when kings either died without heirs or were accused of crimes, or when the emperor ordered kings to divide their kingdoms among their sons. Nevertheless, kings were anxious about their prerogatives, and in 154 the king of Wu convinced six other kings to join him in revolt. Emperor Jing executed Chao Cuo (*Chow Tsoh*), the official who had most vocally advocated reducing the kingdoms, in the hope that this bold move would prevent a war, but the seven kings called out their troops anyway. The king of Wu controlled a wealthy territory with so many natural resources that he was able to minimize the tax burden on his people. In his forty years as king, he had gathered talented men from all over the empire. But perhaps just as important was a personal grudge. Many years earlier his son had gone to the capital to visit his cousin, the imperial heir (and future emperor Jing). The two boys had gotten into an argument over a chess game, and Jing hit his cousin over the head with the chessboard so hard that it killed him. The body was sent back to the king of Wu with apologies, but the incident most certainly did not endear the king to the current emperor, whom he still regarded as the murderer of his son.

The revolt of the seven kingdoms was put down by imperial troops, and after that the threat from independent-minded kings was significantly reduced (though it did not stop two more kings from rebelling, unsuccessfully, in 122). The diminishment of kingdoms continued until there were only eighteen in 108, compared with eighty-six commanderies that same year. On a parallel track was the history of marquisates. These were county-size fiefs that Liu Bang had given to nearly one hundred and fifty of his followers as a reward and a motivation toward continued loyalty. These lands were within commanderies, but marquises were allowed to collect the taxes in their fiefs and keep a percentage. In fact, the rank of marquis was the highest of the twenty ranks—a graded system of social status that Liu Bang borrowed and adapted from Qin administrative practices—and the only one that was inheritable. Han emperors continued to give marquisates to their relatives, to deserving officials, and to surrendered enemy chiefs, but they worked just as hard to curtail these holdings over the long run. Generally by the fourth generation, marquises had been forced to surrender their lands and titles to the central government as a penalty for a crime or because there were no descendants. In fact, in one memorable year, 112, Emperor Wu confiscated over one hundred marquisates.

Most of the information we have about kingdoms comes from histories written in the Han dynasty, but in 1968 an archaeological discovery provided direct evidence of how powerful these political units had once been. Soldiers of the People's Liberation Army found two tombs hidden in a cliff, and these turned out to be the last resting places of the king of the Zhongshan (Liu Sheng, a son of Emperor Jing; d. 114) and his consort Dou Wan. Inside the burial chambers were some 2,800 funeral objects, including bronze vessels inlaid with gold and silver, lacquer ware, silks, figurines, jade objects, mirrors, weapons, chariots, and hundreds of clay pots filled with food and wine. Most impressive of all were two form-fitting jade suits that encased the bodies (see Figure 9). Each was made of over two thousand rectangular pieces of jade, sewn together with gold thread (it was mistakenly thought that jade had the power to prevent decay). If kings were buried in such a lavish manner, we can be sure that they had enormous resources at their disposal.[3]

MILITARY PROBLEMS

With the creation of the Qin and Han empires came the rise of the Xiongnu nomads. These people were considered barbarians by the Chinese because they did not farm or dwell in cities. Instead they lived off of their livestock—mainly horses, cows, and sheep—which they herded from pasture to pasture depending on the season. They were highly mobile, living in tents, and were expert horsemen and warriors. Their ability to strike hard and then disappear made them fearsome enemies, though the real threat came when various Xiongnu groups united in 209 under the leadership of Maodun (*Mau-dwun*; r. 209–174). This new confederation came in response to the First Emperor sending a general north with one hundred thousand men and successfully pushing the Xiongnu out of border regions. The Qin then established commanderies in these new regions and sent in settlers who built roads, garrisons, and walls. Realizing that the Xiongnu needed to reorganize in order to deal with this unprecedented threat to their way of life, Maodun assassinated his father, took over his position as Shanyu (*Shawn-you*, "leader"), and established a stronger, more cohesive federation of Xiongnu clans.

For seven years Maodun prepared his forces, and then in 200 Liu Bang led troops north to try to regain control over a region whose king had just revolted and to expand his territory. This time the Chinese were three hundred thousand strong, but the Xiongnu had even more men, and they defeated the Han army handily (this was the time when Liu Bang was nearly captured). Realizing that his empire had expanded to its practical limits, Liu withdrew and signed a peace treaty with the Xiongnu, establishing a clear border and sending gifts of rice, silk, wine, and a Chinese princess. Maodun thought he was getting the daughter of Liu Bang and Empress Lü as his bride, but the empress protested, and at the last minute another young woman was substituted (see also Document 13 for a later example of a princess being given as a bride to a nomad chieftain).

This "peace and friendship" policy proved effective, and relations between the Han and the Xiongnu were fairly stable for the next half century. In fact, after the death of Liu Bang, Maodun wrote to Empress Lü and proposed marriage: "I am a lonely widowed ruler, born amidst the marshes and brought up on the wild steppes in the land of cattle and horses. I have often come to the border of China wishing to travel in China. Your Majesty is also a widowed ruler living in a life of solitude. Both of us are without pleasures and lack any way to amuse ourselves. It is my hope that we can exchange that which we have for that which we are lacking."[4] The empress felt insulted and wanted to launch an attack in response, but her advisers reminded her that the Han was not in a position to take on the Xiongnu again.

Despite occasional Xiongnu attacks, this same relatively passive approach to foreign relations characterized the quiet reigns of Emperors Jing and Wen—perhaps due in part to the influence of Dowager Empress Dou and her Daoist sympathies. However, in 133, three years after the death of Empress Dou and in the eighth year of his reign, Emperor Wu ordered the first of seven major campaigns against the Xiongnu, several of which mobilized more that one hundred thousand soldiers. The Xiongnu lacked strong leadership at the time, and when a key Xiongnu leader switched sides, the Chinese were able to expand their empire significantly into the west. In fact, in an effort to control the trade route known today as the Silk Road, Chinese armies were sent past the Pamir Mountains to the edges of the Greco-Roman world, some two thousand miles west of the capital.

China's interest in Central Asia was spurred by the remarkable journey of Zhang Qian (*Johng Chyen*), an official who volunteered around 139 to undertake a diplomatic mission to the Yuezhi (*You-eh jer*) people living to the west of the Xiongnu to enlist them as military allies. Zhang was captured by the Xiongnu and held as a prisoner for ten years. Eventually, however, he escaped and continued on his mission, traveling all the way to Bactria (in northwest Afghanistan). The Yuezhi were not willing to come to China's aid, so Zhang turned east to head home. He was captured again by the Xiongnu and again somehow escaped, finally making his way back to the court around 126. He brought information about the western regions, including the fact that Chinese trade goods were already in demand there.

In 120 Chinese forces began pushing southwest into Yunnan (near present-day Burma), and over the next two decades, massive invasions were launched in the northeast (Korean peninsula), the south (Vietnam), and the west (Central Asia). Enormous armies set out nearly every other year to conquer new territories. They established new commanderies where they could, and they made treaties with tributary states when their hold was weaker. Through a combination of diplomacy, gift giving, trade, hostage exchanges, and, of course, military force, the imperial government was successful in dealing with the many non-Chinese peoples on its borders (Emperor Wu's name, given as a posthumous title, means "the Military Emperor"). But as the Daoists well knew, aggressive action in one area might throw off the harmony of the whole, and indeed the balance of power was threatened by two related developments.

The first was that these military campaigns were enormously expensive. Soldiers were not farming when they were fighting or training, and they needed adequate supplies of food, clothing, and equipment in order to perform well. In order to meet these needs, the government had to develop new sources of income. New taxes were introduced, the minting of coins was nationalized, and offices and titles were sold. The government also took over the production of salt and iron—two of the most important and profitable businesses of the day—and tried to stabilize prices by buying grain at harvest time when it was cheap and selling it later when the price had increased (this assistance to farmers netted the authorities a handsome profit). These monopolies were highly controversial, raising serious debate after Emperor Wu's death about the wisdom of having the government interfere so directly in the economy (see Document 14). In any case, it was difficult to sustain such a high level of military expenditures.

The second problem was more personal. Armies must have leaders, and the more successful the general, the more popular he becomes with his troops. It sometimes happens that soldiers become more loyal to their commanders than they are to the government, and Han officials were very wary of this. As a result, talented generals were both valued and feared at court. Perhaps this is one reason that the position of supreme commander—the head of the military branch of the government—often went unfilled after 177. Instead, generals were appointed by the civil authorities for specific campaigns.

One example of such a leader was Li Guang (*Lee Gwong*). Li became a famous general through his unconventional tactics, his cool demeanor under fire, and his amazing ability with a bow. On several occasions his men were vastly outnumbered by the Xiongnu, and he led them to safety. Once, as a wounded prisoner of the Xiongnu, he pretended to be dead and then jumped on a nearby horse, pushing the young rider off and grabbing his bow. He rode some ten miles toward his army at full gallop while shooting several of his pursuers with the bow he had stolen from the Xiongnu boy.

Li was easygoing and generous with his men, and he hated pointless routine and paperwork. The soldiers, not surprisingly, loved him. Court officials and his politically well-connected superiors, however, were not as enthusiastic, and he was never awarded great rank or lavish rewards. In the end, he was kept out of the action in an important battle and then accused of negligence for not showing up on time. Rather than face a court-martial, he committed suicide. Sima Qian reported: "All the officers and men in his army wept at the news of his death, and when word reached the common people, those who had known him and those who had not, old men and young boys alike, were all moved to tears by his fate." Such popularity could make a successful general seem dangerous indeed to the central government.

BUREAUCRACY PROBLEMS

Today we associate the word "bureaucracy" with inefficiency and red tape, but the transition from rule by hereditary aristocrats to salaried professional administrators, or bureaucrats, was one of the great cultural achievements of Chinese civilization. Sons are not always as capable as their fathers, and this is perhaps particularly true of young men who have been raised in an environment of wealth and privilege. It is difficult to fire someone who has strong family connections, even if he is incompetent. Bureaucrats, on the other hand, can be hired on the basis of merit, then rewarded or punished according to their performance in specific duties. Still, as with generals, there is a balance to be struck here. Officials need enough authority to perform their functions, but they also need to be prevented from overstepping their bounds or they may endanger both the emperor and the empire. As Mark Edward Lewis has noted, "The ability to appoint officials, dispatch them to remote cities, maintain control over them at a distance, and remove them when necessary was essential to the creation of a territorial state."[5]

The Qin Empire pioneered the widespread use of bureaucrats, but the Second Emperor apparently gave too little support to his governors, and several early rebels, including Chen She, began by assassinating Qin officials without facing immediate consequences from the imperial authorities. (By contrast, imagine how fast the federal government would become involved after the assassination of a governor or senator in the United States.) On the other hand, Li Si, the chancellor working with Zhao Gao to hide the fact of the First Emperor's death, was operating with far too little oversight. Han rulers, beginning from precedents worked out by the Qin and other states in the Warring States Era, developed an effective system of utilizing bureaucrats, but gaining firm control over these administrators took some time.

The first challenge was finding suitable candidates. Literacy, intelligence, virtue, diligence, and loyalty were all desirable qualities, but where could a ruler locate such persons, especially outside the circle of families that dominated court politics? As early as 196, Liu Bang sent out the following edict:

> At present in the world there are capable men who are wise and able; why should only men of ancient times be capable? The trouble is that the ruler of men does not meet them. . . . If there are any capable gentlemen or sirs who are willing to follow and be friends with me, I can make them honorable and illustrious. . . . Let the foregoing be published to all the world [and transmitted down] to commandery administrators. If any among their people have an excellent reputation and manifest virtue, the officials must personally urge them to come, provide them with chariots and horses, and send them to the courts of the chancellor of state to have written down their accomplishments, their appearance, and their age. If there are such ones and any official does not report them, when this fact becomes known he shall be dismissed.[6]

Note the combination of Confucian ends (recruiting moral administrators) with Legalist means (the threat of dismissal for officials who fail to identify capable men). Though not mentioned in this edict, it was also common in Han times to punish officials if the individuals they recommended turned out to be corrupt.

Similar calls for recommendations went out regularly in the early Han Empire, and by 130 each commandery was expected to put forward two candidates every year. In 124 Emperor Wu established the Imperial Academy as yet another way to identify and train potential officials. Han histories suggest that there were about 120,000 officials serving at the commandery level and above, out of a population of nearly sixty million. Once these men were in place, their actions were evaluated through annual performance reports and the investigations of the censorate branch of the government. After 106 there were thirteen regional inspectors who were appointed to look into the conduct of officials. Administrators were also restrained by the "rule of avoidance," which forbid officials from serving in their native area (to prevent collusion with their relatives). There were promotions and raises for men who did well, and less desirable posts, dismissals, or even criminal prosecutions for those who failed.

Close oversight was important because officials, particularly those at the county level, held tremendous power. They were charged with collecting and transporting taxes, keeping registers of land and people, conscripting men for military and labor service, judging lawsuits, investigating crimes, maintaining irrigation systems and roads, keeping an eye on the economy, officiating at state religious ceremonies, and recommending promising young men as future civil servants. Taxes were set at one-fifteenth of the harvest (later reduced to one-thirtieth), and there was an annual poll tax for every adult as well as for children between the ages of three and fourteen. Able-bodied males from fifteen to fifty-six owed one month every year of unpaid labor service—which could include transporting tax grain, working on construction projects, maintaining roads and canals, and mining—and sometime between the ages of twenty-three and fifty-six they were required to serve two years in the military. Local magistrates were expected to keep track of all this information and submit regular, written reports.

In short, officials were responsible for preserving order among the people and extracting sufficient resources to keep the empire functioning.

Their actions were both supported and restrained by a relatively developed code of laws. As noted in the last chapter, the Han basically adopted the legal system of the Qin, though they claimed to apply the laws less harshly. As Sima Qian put it: "When the Han arose, it lopped off the harsh corners of the Qin code and returned to an easy roundness, whittled away the embellishments and achieved simplicity."[7] Indeed, in 179 Emperor Wen forbid the execution of the families of criminals—a standard Legalist technique of social control—and in 167 he abolished most of the mutilating punishments (see Document 12).

Actually, Qin legal documents—written on bamboo strips and discovered in a tomb in 1975—suggest that the Qin laws themselves were not as harsh as Han historians had implied. For example, failure to show up for labor service seems to have been punished by beatings rather than death, as the story of Chen She's revolt stated. In any case, the penalties that magistrates could impose were serious and included death, beatings, fines, and hard labor (see Document 3). Another tool of social control at the emperor's disposal was the bestowal of one of the twenty ranks—a topic that will be covered in detail in Chapter 4.

Though the bureaucrats were skilled at handling the peasants, merchants presented a special problem. Early Chinese philosophers joined in disparaging businessmen as parasites who did not actually produce anything themselves; they simply took advantage of inefficiencies in distribution to buy low and sell high. (It was only much later that political thinkers realized how essential this function is for a fully developed market economy.) Confucius himself had once said, "The superior man understands what is right; the inferior man understands what is profitable."[8] As a result, merchants had low social status but a great deal of money (perhaps their social position was similar to that of spammers or pornographers today). The problem, as officials saw it, was to prevent merchants from using their money to become powerful and influential. From the time of Liu Bang, merchants were not allowed to wear silk or ride on horseback—though they could easily afford such luxuries—and they were assessed higher taxes. There were later restrictions forbidding them and their descendants from becoming officials, and they were not permitted to own land—which was often a route to respectability. These regulations were not always effective, but merchants were clearly a group to keep under a watchful eye since they were unhappy with the current social structure. It is perhaps not coincidental that all the generals in Chen Xi's (*Chun Shee*) rebel army in 197 were former merchants.

By the nature of their position, bureaucrats were easier to control than kings or generals or consorts. When they displeased the emperor, he simply dismissed them or accused them of crimes. Indeed, ambitious officials hastened to accuse each other of wrongdoing, making politics within the civil branch of the government both complicated and deadly. During the reign of Emperor Wu, the commandant of justice Du Zhou (*Dew Joe*) handled over one thousand cases each year of senior officials accused of crimes, and Emperor Wu executed five of his last seven chancellors. Much of the turmoil was linked to problems originating from the male relatives of Emperor Wu's consorts, including the powerful men who rose to prominence through their connections to Empress Wei Zifu (*Way Dzuh-foo*); in other words, inner court issues could be a major cause of trouble even within the civil branch of government.

Lu Jia (*Loo Jyah*), an official who served under Liu Bang, can provide an example of how important bureaucrats were in aiding the emperor and holding the empire together. In the chaos of the late Qin Empire, Zhao Tuo (*Jau Twoh*), a northerner who was serving as administrator in the southern region stretching from modern Hong Kong down into North Vietnam, revolted and proclaimed himself king of the Southern Yue people who lived there. Liu Bang's forces were not strong enough to take the area; consequently, he sent Lu Jia as an ambassador to grant Zhao official status as the ruler of a tributary state, thus ensuring his continuing cooperation. The Southern Yue were not Chinese, and Zhao Tuo, as their king, had adopted their native dress and distinctive hairstyle. He also considered himself to be equal to Liu Bang, saying, "It is only because I did not begin my uprising in China that I have become the king of this region. If I had been in China, would I not have done just as well as the Han emperor?"[9]

Ambassador Lu Jia stayed among the Southern Yue for several months and argued from Confucian principles that Liu Bang's position as the Son of Heaven was unique and that Zhao Tuo should give up his imperial ambitions, which he did (though his kingdom remained separate from China and outside the Han Empire for another century; only in 111 were the Southern Yue people conquered by the Han and brought into the Chinese cultural sphere). In this case, a single Confucian bureaucrat was able to secure peace on the border, thus freeing up thousands of Liu Bang's soldiers for military action elsewhere.

Lu Jia was opposed to the growing power of Empress Lü's family, and he retired rather than face danger at court. Yet he continued to advise the prime minister informally and was to a large degree responsible for the strategies that overthrew the Lü clan after the death of the empress. Thereafter he rose to high office again, and toward the end of his life he was sent on yet another mission to the Southern Yue when Zhao Tuo impetuously proclaimed himself an emperor. Once again his persuasive arguments convinced Zhao to give up his imperial ambitions and offer his allegiance to the Liu family. Thus Lu Jia not only served the Han emperors as an administrator but also played a key role in helping to fend off problems from the "barbarians" (border peoples) and the inner court alike. Another important contribution was his promotion of Confucianism at court. Liu Bang, as an aggressive military leader, never had much use for the refined morality of Confucian teachings, but Lu Jia was the official who protested that while an empire could be won on horseback, it could not be ruled on horseback. He argued that sovereignty could only be maintained over generations by the principles of benevolence and righteousness, which were precisely what the Qin Empire had lacked. Lu was one of the first Han scholars to work out a Confucian rationale for the empire, a development of tremendous significance.

IMPERIAL IDEOLOGY

As should be quite obvious by now, the position of Chinese emperor was a difficult one, however enviable the personal benefits may have been. The man at the center of the Han Empire had to fend off threats to his power and authority from a variety of sources, many of which originated in regions on the margins of his control—kingdoms on the frontiers, generals in the field, and bureaucrats in distant posts. At times the emperor had to take strong actions to hold the empire together, and though this could be done successfully through a combination of skill, luck, and a certain degree of ruthlessness, handling such challenges on a case-by-case basis was exhausting and left the empire vulnerable if the throne happened to be occupied by a weak or distracted ruler.

As he came to the end of his life, Liu Bang knew that the task of permanent unification was far from over. A few months before his death,

when he was returning to the capital from putting down yet another revolt, Liu happened to pass through his hometown. There he hosted a
feast for its inhabitants and taught the children there to sing a song he
had written himself:

A great wind arose, clouds flew up!
My prestige increasing within the seas, I return to my hometown.
But where will I find valiant warriors to hold the four directions?[10]

A century later, at the time of Emperor Wu, scholars were developing
another tool that would be crucial to the maintenance of empire—a new
attitude toward sovereignty by which emperors were regarded not just as
the lucky descendants of the most successful general of the founding era
but as the cosmic bridge between Heaven and Earth. The terms and
moral concerns of Confucianism were combined with the cosmological
speculations of yin and yang and the Five Phases (the most advanced
"scientific" theories of the day) to form a new system of thought known
today as Han Confucianism.

Dong Zhongshu (*Doong Joong-shoe*), an academician at Emperor Wu's
court, built on the ideas of Lu Jia and others and took the old Zhou dynasty notion of the Mandate of Heaven and extended it so that the emperor was not just the recipient of Heaven's favor; instead, he stood as
an intermediary between humanity and the cosmos. In fact, Dong in-
terpreted the Chinese character for "king" (*wang*, written as 王) as sig-
nifying the way in which the sovereign—represented by the vertical
line—holds together the three parallel realms of Heaven, Earth, and
Man. Given his cosmic position, the emperor could not act despotically,
doing whatever he wished, and Dong's ideas supplied a much-needed
means for officials to check the increasingly autocratic tendencies of Emperor Wu.

Unlike his predecessors, Emperor Wu frequently took the initiative in
ruling, and often overrode the authority of his chancellor. Previous Han
rulers had delegated a large portion of their powers to the chancellor,
who was also the administrator who made criticism of the government
allowable. Other officials might argue with the chancellor, but they could
hardly confront the emperor directly, and criticism became impossible
after government policy began to flow directly from the emperor. In
Dong's solution, advisors urged specific plans on the emperor, not to per-

suade him of the superiority of their own views but to urge him to pattern his actions on Heaven. Referring to the ancient sage-kings, Dong wrote the following in a memorial to the emperor:

> With universal love and free from selfish desires, they spread out their bounties and displayed their humaneness to enrich the people. They established righteous principles and set out behavioral norms to guide the people. Spring is the means by which Heaven generates; humaneness is the means by which the ruler extends his love. Summer is the means by which Heaven brings living things to maturity; virtue is the means by which the ruler nourishes. Frost is the means by which Heaven brings death; punishment is the means by which the ruler corrects.[11]

In exemplifying virtue and aligning themselves with natural patterns (which included the waxing and waning of yin and yang as well as the seasons), emperors could bring peace and harmony to their realms. Indeed, the human and the natural worlds were so intimately connected that political problems could affect the cosmos, and thus an emperor's not properly fulfilling his duties might provoke Heaven's displeasure, as expressed in natural phenomena such as floods, droughts, and strange animals (see Document 12).[12]

This line of reasoning fortified the emperor's position—after all, it is one thing to rebel against a man, even a powerful one; it is quite another to challenge the authority of the Son of Heaven. In other words, opposition to the emperor was more than a crime; it was an affront to the universe. Yet the new ideology was in the interest of officials as well, since it could be used to check the emperor's power. Bureaucrats trying to win support for their ideas could always identify unusual phenomena as portents that required immediate changes in policy or personnel. The combination of a bureaucracy based on merit and an emperor who owed his position to heredity turned out to be both stable and flexible. Because the prestige of the emperor was connected to Heaven, the imperial system could continue to function even if the emperor was underage, disinterested, or incompetent, as long as there were not too many inadequate emperors in a row.

As the role of the emperor became more fully defined, so too did that of his officials. Scholars scoured the historical records to identify a tradition of government service as being the highest calling of moral, educated, civilized men. They celebrated officials of past ages who had spoken their minds forcefully to warn rulers of possible problems, and they disparaged the faults of the Qin—their arrogance and extravagance and dependence on harsh laws. Experts in the Confucian Classics took the lead in all this, and although Emperor Wu was a strong, aggressive ruler in the mold of the First Emperor, early in his reign he established five permanent positions for "Erudite Scholars"—one for each of the Confucian Classics. This gave Confucian scholars a new voice in court debates.

There were also religious developments that buttressed the new authority of the sovereign. Earlier emperors had worshiped the Five Powers (spirits associated with the Five Phases) and set up shrines honoring the dynastic founder, Liu Bang. In 114 Emperor Wu began to worship Earth, and the next year he inaugurated the worship of a new divinity called Grand Unity. About this time he established a Bureau of Music to collect songs and provide musical accompaniment for religious ceremonies. In 110 Emperor Wu performed the legendary Feng and Shan sacrifices on Mount Tai—something not attempted since the time of the First Emperor—and at the foot of the mountain he erected Bright Hall, a building whose architecture reflected the structure of the universe and in which he could perform rituals that would keep the cosmos running smoothly.

When the first Han emperor, Liu Bang, came to the throne, he continued the Qin calendar and adopted Qin beliefs about the cycle of the Five Phases. Thus the Han, like the Qin, regarded Water as its patron phase. But rather than simply taking over from the Qin, scholars began to argue that the Han should adopt the next element in the cycle—Earth—as its patron phase. This change would establish a clear distinction between the Qin and Han empires and signify that the Liu family had the right to rule China not only by virtue of Liu Bang's military conquest but also by the blessings of the cosmos. Scholars argued that the permanence of this change should be reflected in a corresponding change in the dominant phase of the natural cycle of the Five Phases. In 104 Emperor Wu reformed the calendar, asserting that the Han had overcome the phase of Water associated with the Qin and now ruled by the power of Earth. He also declared a new reign title, from which succeeding years would be numbered. The new year was the first of the reign period called the Grand Beginning.

This beginning is perhaps a good point to end this chapter, for much of the ideology developed in the early Han continued until the end of imperial rule in China in the twentieth century. The ideal of government ever after was a unified China under an emperor who was served by bureaucratic officials. Indeed, this was perhaps more than an ideal; it was assumed to be the natural order of things—the norm—and there was considerable unease when China was not unified (something that may still be a factor in ongoing difficulties with Taiwan, which the mainland government considers a breakaway province). Other kingdoms beyond the borders might have a measure of independence, but only if they acknowledged the Chinese emperor as the legitimate ruler of all mankind, directly appointed by cosmic powers. The emperor was the center to whom all on the peripheries owed allegiance, the only person who could keep the civilized world together.

NOTES

1. Burton Watson, trans., *Records of the Grand Historian, Han Dynasty*, 2 vols., rev. ed. (New York and Hong Kong: *Renditions*-Columbia University Press, 1993), 1:44.

2. In counting the number of commanderies here and below, I am including special administrative districts that were set up to govern the capital.

3. See Edmund Capon and William MacQuitty, *Princes of Jade* (New York: E. P. Dutton, 1973).

4. Yü Ying-shih's translation, in "The Hsiung-nu," in *The Cambridge History of Early Inner Asia*, ed. Denis Sinor (New York: Cambridge University Press, 1990), p. 123.

5. Mark Edward Lewis, "Warring States: Political History," in *The Cambridge History of Ancient China: From the Origins of Civilization to 221 B.C.*, ed. Michael Loewe and Edward L. Shaughnessy (New York: Cambridge University Press, 1999), p. 603.

6. Homer H. Dubs, trans., *The History of the Former Han Dynasty*, 3 vols. (Baltimore: Waverly, 1938–55), 1:130–132 (mod.).

7. Watson's translation, *Han*, 2:380.

8. *Analects*, 4.16.

9. Watson's translation, *Han*, 1:226.

10. William H. Nienhauser, Jr., et al., trans., *The Grand Scribe's Records* (Bloomington: Indiana University Press, 2002), 2:82.

11. Sarah A. Queen's translation, in "The Way of the Unadorned King: The Classical Confucian Spirituality of Dong Zhongshu," in *Confucian Spirituality*,

vol. 1, ed. Tu Weiming and Mary Evelyn Tucker (New York: Crossroad Publishing, 2003), p. 309. See Edmund Capon and William MacQuitty, *Princes of Jade* (New York: E. P. Dutton, 1973).

12. There is some indication in the Han sources, however, that explicit Mandate of Heaven claims—as opposed to more general notions of simply being aided by Heaven—were only formally made at the time of Wang Mang, who tried to usurp power from the Liu family and start his own dynasty in the early first century C.E.

CHAPTER 3

TECHNOLOGICAL INNOVATION AND EMPIRE

The Han Empire, which built on and stabilized the accomplishments of the short-lived Qin dynasty, brought a substantial portion of Asia under centralized rule. An empire requires a tremendous amount of money to pay for huge armies, a large bureaucracy, the construction of infrastructure (roads, canals, defensive walls), and an appropriately intimidating capital city. In China, however, there were not large transfers of cash. Although the Chinese did have coins as early as the fifth century B.C.E., the ancient world did not see the same circulation of money that we take for granted today; consequently, the government appropriated grain, cloth, and free labor from the peasants as taxes. The basic principle, however, was the same; soldiers in the field, administrators in their offices, students in schools, and workers at construction sites were not producing food, which meant that someone else had to grow the grain they ate and make the clothes they wore. For much of the world's history, people in many places were living at a subsistence level—that is to say, they barely produced enough of the necessities of life to feed and clothe and house themselves. Historians use the term "civilization" in a particular way to refer to societies in which there is enough surplus to support specialized occupations (craftsmen, priests, merchants), a ruling class, a state government, and cities. Yet the material resources required by an empire go far beyond even this.

Think, for instance, of the underground chambers filled with seven thousand life-size, armed, terra-cotta soldiers guarding the First Emperor's tomb, which itself was a huge complex about a mile to the west of the underground army. The construction of the terra-cotta army would have taken thousands of man-hours (though certainly much less than the tomb itself), yet the First Emperor could afford to simply cover it over and leave it. We are not exactly sure what it was intended to accomplish—To protect the emperor's tomb from evil spirits? To extend his empire into the world of the dead?—but it was certainly not built to impress any of his contemporaries, and the effort and wealth that went into it could have been redirected toward projects that had some tangible benefit in the land of the living. The resources at the First Emperor's disposal as he conquered China, expanded its borders, and established the system of commanderies and counties were staggering. An even better example is Liu Bang's campaign in 201, in which he led an army of 320,000 men north to fight against the Xiongnu nomads. How much do 320,000 soldiers eat in a single day? Something dramatic must have happened in Chinese farming so that each person growing food could produce enough to feed several others working at other tasks. As we shall see later, the Chinese made impressive advances in military weaponry that aided conquest and defense, but the basis of any successful empire was increased agricultural production.

Agricultural innovations continued throughout the four centuries of Han rule. This steady progress in agricultural science and technology is significant for three reasons. First, as the population grew, it was necessary for farm production to grow even faster; otherwise, the available surplus would have been inadequate to keep an empire going. Second, as we saw in the conflict between the imperial state and the kingdoms in the last chapter, the natural tendency in large empires is for local elites to seek power at the expense of the central government by diverting taxes normally paid to the central government and funneling them into the military and economic resources in their area. It was this very process that eventually brought down the Han dynasty, but the empire was able to last as long as it did only because of the sophisticated farming techniques of its citizens—a good portion of which went to support the emperor, his administrators, and his troops. And third, modes of agriculture had a tremendous impact on the daily lives of the Han Chinese, determining what they wore and ate and how they spent their time. Truly, as several imperial edicts of the time stated, "Agriculture is the foundation of the Empire" (see Figure 10).

AGRICULTURAL TECHNOLOGY

Farming families in Han China were typically households of four or five people—two parents and their children—and together they worked plots of about eleven acres. In northern China, farmers grew wheat and millet (a food most commonly encountered in the United States today as the small, round grain in birdseed), while rice was the primary crop in southern China. Of course, families often had pigs, mulberry trees (to feed silkworms), and gardens to care for as well. Farming then, as now, was a difficult way of life, as can be seen in this memorial written in 178:

> They till the land in spring, hoe in summer, harvest in autumn, and store in winter. Besides, they have to cut wood for fuel, work in the government buildings, and render labor service [part of their tax obligation]. In the spring they cannot escape the wind and dust; in the summer they cannot escape the heat; in the autumn they cannot escape the chilling rain; and in the winter they cannot escape the cold. Throughout the four seasons they do not have a single day of rest.[1]

And this description of life applied to the vast majority of the people of the Han (as opposed to the United States today, where less than 2 percent of the population is engaged in agriculture).

Yet the unrelenting physical labor required could have been even harder and far less productive if it were not for several innovations developed from the fourth century B.C.E. to the second century C.E. We can note many of these advances by following the course of farm work through a single year. The first task was to prepare the soil for planting. This task required picks, spades, and plows, and by Han times, these tools were generally made of iron, which was much more suitable than bronze (see Figure 11). (Although iron makes for stronger tools and iron ore is relatively abundant, iron production usually followed that of bronze in ancient civilizations because iron-working requires more sophisticated techniques of metallurgy.) Metal workers refined the shape of plows so that they became better at cutting through the soil, and then eventually attached moldboards, which simultaneously lifted and turned over the soil and reduced friction. An adjustable vertical strut regulated the depth of the furrow, making Han plows far more sophisticated than those employed anywhere else in the world. Cutting a furrow in the ground required more force than manpower alone could provide, and the use of oxen became more widespread as well.

In ancient times, farmers sowed crops by broadcasting—as they walked across their fields, they threw the seed by hand. This resulted in poorly spaced crops and considerable waste (not to mention well-fed wild birds).

The Han solution was to plant seeds in deep furrows between broad ridges. This arrangement protected the young sprouts from both too much rain and too little—both were dangers in North China—and allowed a degree of crop rotation, since the ridges of one year would become the furrows of the next. The Han even invented the world's first seed drill—a plowlike device that was pulled by an animal and that dribbled the seed directly into furrows at a controlled rate. Farmers in the south grew rice in paddies, which were basically flooded fields. Han farmers carefully timed the planting of different types of crops, and they practiced crop rotation and planted multicrop systems (where more than one kind of plant is grown in the same field), alternating cereals with nitrogen-fixing legumes likes beans.

As the plants grew, they were carefully watered, weeded (with iron hoes), and fertilized. The Chinese were so economical that they collected the contents of their own outhouses to use in the fields as fertilizer. Human sewage, called nightsoil, provided nutrients for crops, but it had to be fermented and treated carefully to reduce the spread of disease. (The widespread use of nightsoil is one reason the Chinese today generally avoid raw foods—nearly everything is cooked at high temperatures in a wok—and boil their water before it is drinkable.) Yet the combination of efficient sewage disposal and greater crop yields more than made up for the health risks.

When the grain ripened, it was harvested with iron sickles, threshed (to remove the grain from the straw), and then winnowed (to separate the grain and the chaff). The last of these procedures was accomplished in some parts of Han China by a rotary-fan winnowing machine, essentially a blower operated by a hand crank—the first use of a crank in history. Elsewhere in the world, farmers would wait for a strong wind, and then they would throw the grain into the air with shovels or large, flat baskets so that the lighter chaff would be blown away.

Transportation became an issue after the grain was harvested, and the world's first efficient harnessing of horses was developed in China in the fourth century B.C.E. Previously, horses had been attached to carts or chariots by the "throat and girth" harness, in which a horse pulled against a strap around its neck. Needless to say, an arrangement in which the harder the horse pulled, the less it was able to breathe, seriously limited the amount of work that could be done. The Chinese invented the trace harness, with a breast strap that put pressure on the horse's chest bone (sternum) rather than its windpipe. Shortly before the Han dynasty, the horse collar was invented, which allowed the horse to pull even greater loads more efficiently. During the Han era, the wheelbarrow came into general use. It may be a simple concept, but it enabled a single individual to move around loads of a hundred pounds or more with ease.

Other tasks undertaken by farming families included food processing, the spinning and weaving of textiles, metalworking, house building, gardening, the raising of animals, and the manufacture and repair of pottery and tools. Making cloth was usually the responsibility of women, and although most people wore coarse clothes of hemp, the Chinese had known the secrets of silk manufacture (sericulture) for centuries. But it was only during the Han that delicate production of this marvelous fabric—involving the care of silkworms, the need for mulberry leaves to feed them, the complicated process of boiling and unraveling the cocoons, and the spinning of the cloth—became widespread throughout China. As early as the first century B.C.E., some of the silk produced in China made its way west along the Silk Road to the Roman Empire, where its origin must have been mysterious to the wives of senators who were able to enjoy such luxury goods.

The government, realizing the importance of agriculture, encouraged farming in many ways. The basic tax rate was low (one-thirtieth of the harvest, although tenant farmers were often forced to pay half their crops to their landlord, who then paid the low taxes himself), and the government undertook many large irrigation projects. As the state of Qin was conquering its rivals, one nervous ruler sent a hydraulic engineer named Zheng Guo (*Jeng Gwo*) to the king of Qin, hoping that his extravagant schemes to build a huge canal would bankrupt the powerful state. When this deception was discovered, Zheng assured the king that his ideas could actually work, and indeed the Zheng Guo canal, completed in 246 (the same year the First Emperor took the throne), turned out to be a major success in increasing the agricultural production of Qin. In the Han dynasty as well, the state ordered the construction of dozens of canals, along with dikes and reservoirs, which brought regular irrigation—and better transportation—to over a million acres.

The government opened up new lands and encouraged the resettlement of hundreds of thousands of farmers in the underpopulated areas of the north and northwest through tax breaks, grants of food and seed grain, and loans of animals and tools. In classic Confucian style, the emperor encouraged his people by example, and he himself plowed a furrow in a ceremonial field at the beginning of each new year (see Figure 12). To lead and inspire the female populace, his empress engaged in ceremonial sericultural activities. The government also claimed to benefit farmers through seizing control of the critical industries of iron and salt. By manipulating the market through the "ever-normal granaries," they attempted to regularize prices by buying grain at harvest time to keep the farmers' asking-price high, and then selling the grain later in the year to reduce prices when farmers had to buy foodstuffs themselves. These programs, however, were often criticized as more concerned with making money for the government than improving the lives of ordinary peasants (see Document 14).

How did all this compare with farming elsewhere at the time? Most people know that imperial China led the world in technological innovation and sophistication, and that inventions originating in China—such as paper, gunpowder, and the compass (the latter two came a bit later, but paper was developed during the Han Empire)—changed the course of global history. Agriculture also followed this pattern. The idea of a crank—a handle attached to a wheel—may seem simple enough, but no one in Europe thought of it until the ninth century C.E. Similarly, while wheelbarrows were used in China during the Han dynasty, they did not appear in the West until the thirteenth century.

The story is the same with most of the techniques mentioned above. The breast-strap harness and horse collar show up in the West in the thirteenth century. Cast iron—which can be poured into molds and mass-produced—was known to the Chinese since the fourth century B.C.E. but was not readily available in Europe until the fourteenth century C.E. (though Europe did use wrought iron, that is, iron that was hammered and shaped into individual tools while hot). And several related developments such as double-action piston bellows (which produced a steady stream of air), water-powered bellows, and the production of steel from cast iron were common in China a thousand years before they were used in the West. Europeans still sowed their fields by broadcasting seed as late as the eighteenth century, about the time when the integrated farming methods of Han China were finally adopted in the West. Europeans began using plows with curved metal moldboards and winnowing rotary fans, both of which seem to have been copied directly from Chinese examples. In the seventeenth century, Chinese plows were first

brought to Holland by Dutch sailors, and winnowing fans were introduced into Europe from China in the early eighteenth century by
Swedish travelers and French Jesuits.

MILITARY TECHNOLOGY

As mentioned above, taxes on the harvest were relatively light, but
that is not the whole story. The state also levied an annual poll tax, to
be paid in cash, that was assessed on every adult fifteen and older (and
at a reduced rate for children between three and fourteen). But the tax
burden that was most dreaded was the labor obligation. From the age of
fifteen until the age of fifty-six, each Chinese man was required to give
a month of labor to the government, without pay, every year. Someone
had to dig the canals, build the roads, repair the dikes, mine iron ore, defend against bandits, and transport the tax grain, and it was the taxpay-
ers themselves. These work duties took farmers away from their land and
families, and if the call came at the wrong season, farm work might be
seriously disrupted.

In addition to labor service, men (and occasionally women) were conscripted for military duty. At some time during those thirty-three years
of obligation, all men were required to spend two years in the army—
one year in their home region and another either at the capital or at the
frontier (though two-year tours of duty were probably a welcome reduction from the decades of fighting that had involved hundreds of thousands of men in the conflicts leading up to the unification under the Qin
and the civil war preceding the establishment of the Han dynasty). There
were some military professionals, but the majority of fighting men were
farmer-soldiers who were fulfilling their civil obligations. For two years
they were given food, clothing, and equipment, but no pay. Women did
not sit idle while their menfolk served in the army and on labor projects.
Sources suggest that while women took part in combat during times of
military emergency, they are more typically shown contributing to the
state through the production of cloth. The importance of textile manufacture is clear in a state where cloth could be used in place of money to
pay fines and taxes. Families that produced large amounts of cloth were
at times excused from conscript labor duty. The state may also have
drafted women on an irregular basis for their sewing skills, as the First
Emperor of Qin did when he dispatched fifteen thousand women to Yue

to sew army uniforms. After the founding of the Han, the government faced three types of military challenges: renegade Chinese kings, nomadic Xiongnu to the north, and the expansion of Chinese control west over the Silk Road, northeast to Korea, and south toward Vietnam. Particularly under Emperor Wu (r. 141–87), China increased its territory dramatically, following victories in the field with tens of thousands of relocated settlers and military colonies that fed and supported the soldiers. What made Chinese armies so successful in building up and holding such a large empire?

The first answer is organization. The Chinese were able to muster armies of tens of thousands, with adequate equipment and provisions, and in so doing they could overwhelm most of their enemies. In addition, they fought according to tactics that had been developed during the Warring States Era—that is, deploying large numbers of infantry surrounded by chariots and supported by cavalry. Although these tactics were not always effective in fighting the Xiongnu horsemen, who were much more mobile (the techniques the Chinese had developed for besieging cities were of no use in attacking people who simply folded up their tents and retreated into the desert), massive military campaigns did have an impact on the nomads, and the combination of war, trade, diplomacy, and bribery went a long way toward neutralizing the threat from the north.

Another element in Chinese military strength was the building up of their infrastructure. During the Han, about twenty thousand miles of roads were constructed, which carried not only merchants and travelers, but more importantly officials, reports, orders, grain, and soldiers. A sophisticated communication network was essential in making sure that troops were in place and properly provisioned. Records written on bamboo slips that survived in the dry climate of the northwest for two thousand years have given modern scholars a good idea of how that area was defended. There were long lines of fortifications with watchtowers and walls (though not the massive stone structure seen today in photos of the Great Wall, which was built in the sixteenth century). Soldiers on guard duty would go out on patrol and look for signs of the enemy, and they had an elaborate system of signals for passing news from tower to tower—flags and smoke by day, torches by night, and bonfires in emergencies. The soldiers worked with police dogs, checked passports, and compared suspicious persons to written descriptions of wanted fugitives. They were also responsible for searching out and recording the names of any travelers crossing the borders.

Finally, the Chinese gained some military advantages from their weapons. As late as the founding of the Qin dynasty, most weapons were made of bronze, but during the Han period, iron and steel spears, swords, axes, and knives became more common (and iron swords could be twice as long as the old bronze models). The Chinese mastery of cast iron also allowed for the mass production of weapons from molds, long before such techniques were used in the West. Personal armor was created from small plates of iron that were riveted or tied together with cords. The Chinese employed bows and arrows, as well as catapults, but their most fearsome piece of equipment was the crossbow (see Figure 1). This is a horizontal bow set on a gunlike stock, with a mechanism to hold the string in the cocked position until it is released by a trigger. Unlike regular bows, crossbows can be kept ready to fire and aimed without constant pulling. They can also shoot much farther and more forcefully. The trigger mechanisms, made of bronze, were masterpieces of engineering and were so precisely manufactured that China's enemies had difficulty copying them. Crossbows had been in China since the Warring States Era, but the Han continued to refine them, creating some that were as large as artillery pieces and others that could shoot more than one bolt at a time. They also developed graduated sighting scales and grid sights for more precise aiming. Although there were some scattered examples of primitive crossbows among the Greeks, there was really nothing like the Chinese crossbow in the West until the tenth century, when it revolutionized warfare in Europe (and even then the idea may have been imported from China, through a Central Asian people known as the Khazars).[2]

Although warfare was a constant element of the Han Empire, by the end of the reign of Emperor Wu, the nature of the military had changed from what it had been during the Warring States Era (403–221) and the Qin dynasty (221–207). Generals could no longer act independently of the king or emperor while in the field, and in any case, they tended to be drawn from the imperial consort clans. Because the wars were generally in more distant places, universal conscription of large infantry armies no longer made sense. Emperor Wu therefore began to recruit volunteers who could train for more than two years and become professionals in horse riding and crossbow shooting—the types of skills needed in border warfare against nomadic peoples. The men who were willing to spend their lives in frontier garrisons often came from the ranks of convicts and non-Chinese peoples. Gradually China moved from a situation of continuous warfare among more or less equal states to the imperial system in which a centralized government firmly controlled the military and concentrated most of its efforts on civil administration. This basic trend became evident at the time of Emperor Wu and continued through most of Imperial Chinese history.[3]

SCIENTIFIC INNOVATIONS

It is important to recognize that our modern conception of science—secular inquiry into natural phenomena based on careful observation, mathematical analysis, and experimentation, carried on by a wide community connected through regular publishing, collaboration, and supporting institutions like research laboratories and universities—is foreign to early China (and to the rest of the ancient world, for that matter). Yet there were some Chinese thinkers who were interested in questions that we regard as scientific today, and some of these men made important discoveries or invented useful devices. They were generally working on their own, however, and their worldviews were not quite like those held by scientists today.

In early China, philosophers were interested in the way that things change over time. Two of the most widely accepted theories were the interaction of yin and yang, and the succession of the Five Phases. The first of these—often represented by the familiar symbol of a circle with white on one side and black on the other, divided by an S-shaped line—suggests that everything in the world is composed of a combination of two opposite forces: yang, which is characterized as light, active, initiating, and male; and yin, which is dark, passive, persevering, and female. When the yin level in a person, situation, or thing becomes too high, there will be a natural correction by which the yang force reasserts itself. And after a period of increasing yang, the power of yin will return again. In this way, the natural rhythm of change is something like the swings of a pendulum. For example, some physicians in early China viewed sickness as the result of imbalances in yin and yang, and a skilled doctor could accelerate the process of healing by prescribing medicines or foods that were especially potent in supplying the necessary opposite.

In a similar fashion, other contrasting influences in life might also seek equilibrium. An early Chinese saying was *le ji sheng bei*—"When happiness reaches an extreme, sorrow follows"—and many Chinese sought to live their lives in accordance with such wisdom. For instance, when Emperor Wen of the Han appointed Zhou Bo (*Joe Bwo*) chancellor—a very high position with a generous cash payment and a large salary—a friend warned him that "Before long, disaster will surely come upon you."[4] Zhou thereupon resigned his position, hoping to avoid the trouble and downfall that seemed inevitable.

Experts in yin-yang theory wrote texts that recommended appropriate days for various activities and warned of bad luck if their advice for harmonizing natural forces was not followed. Eventually their ideas became connected to the second proto-scientific school, that of the Five Phases. Like yin-yang theorists, experts in Five Phase cosmology explained the process of change as stemming from a regular succession of natural forces that replaced each other by conquest: Fire is extinguished by Water, which is dammed by Earth, which is split by Wood (wooden tools, that is), which is chopped by Metal, which is melted by Fire, and so on. Five Phase theorists put forward this cycle to explain dynastic change—since the Zhou dynasty was thought to have ruled by the power of Fire, the Qin adopted Water as their patron phase, with its associated number and color. Emperor Wu of the Han in turn proclaimed his dynasty's affinity for Earth in 104 with great fanfare.

Seasons, directions, tastes, colors, planets, internal organs, feelings, etc., all became associated with particular phases, and this theory explained how they interacted. The following are a few of the associations developed in early China:

	Wood	**Fire**	**Earth**	**Metal**	**Water**
Seasons	spring	summer	—	autumn	winter
Numbers	eight	seven	five	nine	six
Directions	east	south	center	west	north
Colors	green	red	yellow	white	black
Animals	sheep	fowl	ox	dog	pig
Planets	Jupiter	Mars	Saturn	Venus	Mercury
Organs	spleen	lungs	heart	liver	kidneys
Govt. Ministers	Agriculture	War	Works	Interior	Justice[5]

Some of this makes sense—for instance, it is plausible to connect Fire with the color red and the season of summer; it might be appropriate for a ruler to focus on agriculture in the spring; judicial executions seem to fit the bleak winter season (even in Rome, quite independently, the red planet Mars was associated with the god of war). Yet the connections here are based on correlation rather than causation. Furthermore, all things that belonged to one category were linked, so that when one component was affected, everything else in that category was affected as well. This belief gave rise to the notion of "stimulus and response" (*ganying*), which suggested that a drought (yang), for example, could be remedied by commanding women (yin) to congregate in public, because rain would be stimulated in response to their yin. Once the basic cycle was determined, the real effort went into trying to fit all sorts of phenomena into the appropriate category of correspondence. Later thinkers added further refinements—more in keeping with the Han's professed interest in ruling by right rather than might—by arguing that the proper sequence was not one of conquest but production: Wood produces Fire, which produces Earth (in the form of ashes), which produces Metal (mined from earth), which produces Water (the Chinese had noticed the condensation that collects on metal tools), which produces Wood, which in turn produces Fire again.

Ideas concerning correlative cosmology such as the ones described above began in the Warring States Era among independent philosophers and then gained influence with scholars in the court of the First Emperor. Though early Han rulers seemed less interested in such speculations, these theories were further developed and combined with Confucianism at the time of Emperor Wu. The men behind these ideas wanted to find connections between man and nature, heaven and earth, and past and present. Although some of their observations may sound a bit strange today, Chinese thinkers were motivated by the desire to understand man's place in nature and history; consequently, they recorded detailed observations of the world around them. Though Chinese civilization is frequently (and erroneously) characterized as lacking in a scientific tradition, it is worth noting that in recording their observations, thinkers engaged in linking human history to cosmological speculation made advances in many of the fields we today classify as science, including astronomy, biology, geology, mathematics, and meteorology.

For instance, Chinese intellectuals—many in the service of the emperor—charted the heavens and observed the movements of the moon and planets, making notations of eclipses, novas, comets, and meteors. They constructed an accurate calendar of 365¼ days, which they reconciled with the 355-day lunar year (twelve months of 29.5 days each—the time from full moon to full moon). They noted the existence of sunspots and determined that Saturn made a complete cycle through the sky in thirty years (modern astronomers fix its orbit at 29.46 years). They built carefully calibrated instruments that, while not telescopes, allowed astronomers to measure the progress of heavenly bodies with great accuracy. Some of these devices were even hydraulically powered, so they tracked the apparent motion of the heavens through the night. They also hypothesized that the sun is the source of the moon's light, that tides are caused by the moon, and that solar eclipses are the result of the moon obscuring the sun. And they figured out that rain and snow do not originate in the sky, but come from the moisture in soil and surface water, which evaporates into the atmosphere and then is condensed into clouds and precipitated downward. Han thinkers built accurate water clocks and invented paper, which made it easier and eventually more economical to preserve and transmit communications of all kinds—from philosophical writings to government documents to poetry. They calculated pi at 3.1622 and observed that snowflakes always have six sides (something not noticed in the West until about 1600). They identified and catalogued hundreds of plants with medicinal properties.

The achievements of the early Chinese are impressive, but presenting these innovations in terms of modern science can be somewhat misleading. Clearly, Han thinkers were working from within a different worldview. For instance, Zhang Heng (*Johng Hung*; 78–139 C.E.) is often credited with inventing the world's first seismograph. In fact, he did make an earthquake detection device, but he was not exactly a "scientist"; he was an official who also had interests in poetry, painting, mathematics, cartography, and astronomy. The instrument he created consisted of a large, covered bronze jar with eight dragon heads arranged at equal intervals around the upper edge. Each dragon held a bronze ball in its mouth, and around the base were eight open-mouthed frogs. Inside was a weighted, balanced cylinder. When an earthquake struck, the shock waves would rock the cylinder, which would then strike a trigger mechanism that would cause one of the dragons to drop its ball into the frog's mouth below (see Figures 13 and 14). Here is the account from the *History of the Later Han*:

On one occasion one of the dragons let fall a ball from its mouth though no perceptible shock could be felt. All the scholars at the capital were astonished at this strange effect occurring without any evidence of an earthquake to cause it. But several days later a messenger arrived bringing news of an earthquake in Longxi [Gansu, about 400 miles away in the northwest]. Upon this everyone admitted the mysterious power of the instrument. Thenceforth it became the duty of the officials of the Bureau of Astronomy and Calendar to record the directions from which earthquakes came.[6]

Zhang's interest in earthquake detection, however, was not the outgrowth of curiosity about geology. Rather, it was directly connected to theories of correlative cosmology, which envisioned potent links between the human, natural, and heavenly spheres. Earthquakes, like eclipses and droughts, were thought to be portents—signs of Heaven's displeasure at human wrongdoing. By quickly identifying the site of an earthquake, the emperor could immediately send inspectors to investigate the bureaucratic misdeeds and corruption that might have been the cause of such a natural disaster. Only by dealing forcefully with administrative problems could the emperor fulfill his cosmic function of preserving the natural harmony that ought to exist between Heaven and Earth.

In bringing this chapter to a conclusion, it seems fitting to enumerate once again the advances made by Han craftsmen and artisans. Michèle Pirazzoli-t'Serstevens has conveniently summarized the main technological innovations in the Han Empire as follows:

The cog-wheel, crank, odometer, water mill, caliper rule with decimal scale (used by Chinese artisans from the beginning of the first century C.E. at the latest), paper, the wheelbarrow, sternpost, mechanical seeder and the winnower with rotary wings. Besides these inventions, advances were made in older techniques, unknown outside China at the time, like silk and lacquer work, bronze casting and the production of steel, not to mention the crossbow and breast harness, which were exclusively Han.[7]

Robert Temple would add such inventions as the belt drive, the chain pump, the suspension bridge, the discovery of blood circulation and hormones, negative numbers, and decimal fractions.[8]

This is an impressive list, which demonstrates the intelligence and creativity of Han thinkers, but why would such inventions matter to the founding of the Han Empire and the establishment of imperial China? They are important for three reasons. The first is that technological innovation allowed for the material prosperity that put the empire on firm footing and paid for the cost of troops, bureaucracy, and imperial splendor. The second is that the military power of the empire was increased by improvements in weaponry and organization. And the third is that there was tremendous symbolic value in many of the discoveries of Han scholars. As we saw in the previous chapter, the authority of the Han emperors was tied to their claims to mediate between Heaven, Earth, and Man. The regulation of the calendar, for example, was essential to the promotion of agriculture, but it was also symbolic of the emperor's connection to Heaven itself.

NOTES

1. Cho-yun Hsu, *Han Agriculture: The Formation of Early Chinese Agrarian Economy (206 B.C.–A.D. 220)*, ed. Jack L. Dull (Seattle: University of Washington Press, 1980), p. 161. See Document 10 for a longer excerpt.

2. See Robert Temple, *The Genius of China: 3,000 Years of Science, Discovery, and Invention* (New York: Simon and Schuster, 1989), pp. 218–224.

3. See Mark Edward Lewis, *Writing and Authority in Early China* (Albany: State University of New York Press, 1999), pp. 351–352.

4. *Shiji*, 57.2072; see Burton Watson, trans., *Records of the Grand Historian, Han Dynasty*, 2 vols., rev. ed. (New York and Hong Kong: *Renditions*-Columbia University Press, 1993), 1:373.

5. For a longer list of correlations, see Theodore De Bary and Irene Bloom, eds., *Sources of Chinese Tradition: From Earliest Times to 1600*, 2nd ed. (New York: Columbia University Press, 1999), p. 348.

6. Joseph Needham, *Science and Civilization in China* (Cambridge: Cambridge University Press, 1959), 3:627–628.

7. Michèle Pirazzoli-t'Serstevens, *The Han Dynasty*, trans. Janet Seligman (New York: Rizzoli, 1982), p. 210. Spelling Americanized.

8. Temple, pp. 54, 56, 58, 123, 127, 141, 142.

CHAPTER 4

SOCIAL CHANGE IN HAN TIMES

When the king of Qin gained dominion over all of China and established his own dynasty in 221 B.C.E., he dissolved the system of hereditary aristocratic ranks that had prevailed in China for centuries. Aristocrats suddenly found themselves stripped of their titles, and the once independent and often warring kingdoms now fell under the administration of centrally appointed, non-hereditary officials. But for centuries already, observers had witnessed the gradually weakening, ever more corrupt, and increasingly dysfunctional nature of the now-rejected system of entitlement instituted by the Zhou dynasty almost a millennium earlier. Under the Qin, men (and to a lesser extent, women) distinguished themselves not by birth but largely through their achievements in warfare and agriculture, and they could obtain non-hereditary titles and privileges within a system of ranks. But when the energetic and visionary First Emperor died in 210, his son proved unequal to the task of imperial rule, and the Qin Empire fell three years later. In 202, the first Han emperor, Liu Bang, reorganized the administrative units of the empire, adopting for central China the Qin-dynasty system of commanderies—controlled by centrally-appointed governors—and for east and north China, kingdoms (see Map 2).

The social history of the Han is bound to the administrative structure of the empire. It is important to keep in mind that the founder of the Han retained some of the institutional features of the Qin but with the crucial difference that the Han ruler reestablished the system of hereditary entitlement that had been abandoned in the Qin by making members of the imperial family kings. Liu Bang combined this new royalty with a meritocratic bureaucracy and a meritocratic system of ranks. This system—officials appointed on the basis of merit serving a ruling dynasty founded on and maintained according to hereditary privilege—became the blueprint for state organization used throughout most of imperial China (see Figure 15).

We can describe the civil service as a meritocratic bureaucracy because, at least in theory, officials were hired and fired according to their abilities and performance, and because the positions were not hereditary. In addition to the civil service, however, the Han instituted another system of ranks similar to one used in the Qin, which was open to nearly all men of the empire. According to this system, all imperial subjects—apart from slaves and criminals—were entitled to aristocratic titles graded into twenty ranks above that of commoner. (In addition to being the highest, the rank of marquis was the only one that was inheritable.) The emperor frequently bestowed ranks on ordinary men as gifts (usually in celebration of some happy occasion in the imperial family) or as a reward for merit, and at times even offered them for sale.

In general, the first through eighth ranks were for the general public. Ranks above the eighth order were for officials, though these ranks were distinct from civil service positions that involved actual duties. In the Qin, ordinary individuals with no rank were called *shiwu* (*sure-woo*), which can be roughly translated as "rank and file." (In the Han, the term was only used to denote individuals who had been stripped of their ranks.) Ordinary people were allowed to accumulate titles by purchase or imperial bestowal, but could not generally rise above the eighth rank. The great majority of ranks were given to men, while their wives' ranks corresponded to that of their husbands. Very occasionally women received ranks—usually for merit, but also when there was no heir to receive a deceased husband's title.

Holding an aristocratic rank was no empty honor, and preferential treatment, while not great for those at the bottom of the scale, increased with rank. Those who held rank were exempt from punishment by enslavement and, in the case of the twelve higher orders, were free from taxation as well as military and labor services owed the state. If convicted of a crime, titleholders also received more lenient treatment than ordinary criminals. In addition, individuals with aristocratic rank could relinquish their title in return for a reduction in state punishments. Beginning with the ninth order, privileges included exemption from state service and the privilege of wearing the hat of the imperial Liu clan. Only those of the twentieth rank could pass on their title to descendants, and their title also conferred upon them landed estates and the right to collect and retain a portion of the taxes from their estates. (For a list of the twenty ranks, see the appendix at the end of this chapter.)

Because of the biases of early Chinese texts, most available information concerns people connected with the imperial family and the educated elite, and the majority of these people are male. While sources concerning commoners, women, and slaves are far more limited, an effort will be made to show how these groups fared in the early days of the Chinese empire. We shall begin at the apex of society with an examination of the relationship between the imperial family who lived in the capital and other nobles who resided in the kingdoms during Han times.

ARISTOCRATS

The emperor granted kingdoms to all of his sons apart from the imperial heir apparent, who would succeed his father as emperor. The eldest son of a king and queen inherited the kingdom, while his brothers inherited the position of marquis. The emperor's sisters and daughters were titled either senior princess or princess, ranks equivalent to that of king and marquis, respectively, and were provided with landed estates. Their privileges included the power to collect taxes from their populace (a portion of which they could retain for their own use), to draw on the natural resources of their domains, and to choose a reduction of noble rank in lieu of suffering punishment for crimes. The two primary duties of the kings were to collect taxes and to raise and train armies for the use of the central government. Because they enjoyed certain legal and economic advantages, kings faced the temptation to abuse their special status, which in turn placed them under the intense scrutiny of an increasingly suspicious central government. Han historical sources frequently focus substantial attention on the scandalous behavior of kings as well as on imperial efforts—at times paranoid and at times justifiable—to control them. Until 145, kings were empowered to appoint their own officials, but were eventually stripped of this right when their interests began to collide with and challenge the will of the central government. Thus, after 100, there was little distinction between the administrative structure of commanderies (headed by a centrally appointed bureaucrat) and kingdoms (headed by kings who were imperial kin).

Biographical accounts of wayward young aristocrats expose another tension generated by the new social system of the Han dynasty, namely, the contradictions inherent in a political system in which some positions of authority and privilege were inherited while others were granted on the basis of merit. In theory, the merit of a potential heir to the throne was as important as his lineage. Princes therefore needed to be educated, just as ordinary boys who hoped to enter the ranks of officialdom had to prove themselves worthy of the positions they would eventually fill. But in reality, for anyone related to the imperial family, staying out of trouble was probably sufficient to maintain a secure grasp on a noble title. Clearly, even in cases where kings violated the law, the emperor often intervened and exempted them from punishment.

Confucius once said that in trying to appraise a person, if you "discover what brings him content . . . can the man's real worth remain hidden from you?"[1] Analyzing a person's preferences in play and other leisure activities became a standard approach to character assessment in the early histories. Han historians repeatedly cited aristocratic adolescents' fondness for gambling, hunting, cockfighting, and dog and horse racing as evidence of their moral deficiencies. By the early Han, certain pleasurable pastimes had become so intimately associated with aristocratic youth and the wealthy elite that the biography of Liu An (*Leo Awn*), king of Huainan (d. 122), begins by stating that he did not enjoy "shooting, hunting, and dashing about with dogs and horses." Earnest attempts to discourage young Han rulers from devoting themselves to frivolous pursuits begin to appear early in the reign of Emperor Wu, for it was he who seemed more intent than any of his predecessors on using his imperial privileges to pursue private pleasure.

For example, in approximately 135, when Emperor Wu was in late adolescence, the poet Sima Xiangru (*Sue-ma Shyang-roo*) composed "Sir Fantasy," a rhapsody illustrating the leisure activities appropriate to a youthful sovereign. In this piece, Sima depicts the Son of Heaven as first enjoying himself in pleasures like hunting, but then finally rejecting such delights to pursue a rigorous program of classical study and Confucian self-cultivation:

> Now, when I am unoccupied, blessed with a moment free from attending to the concerns of the state and with a day at my disposal, following Heaven's autumnal work of slaying and reaping, from time

to time I take my ease in this hunting park. But I fear that in generations to come, those who follow me in this pursuit will become lost in excess with no hope of turning back. This is no way to assure to dynastic continuity or to forge a solid foundation for future achievements!

By contrast, Liu Sheng (*Leo Shung*), king of Zhongshan and brother of Emperor Wu, argued that it was virtually a king's duty to occupy himself with pleasure. He thus ridiculed his industrious brother, the king of Zhao, for spending "all his time doing the work of his own clerks and officials."[2]

Aristocratic upbringing at its worst seems to have encouraged in elite youth a series of behaviors that ranged from the dissolute to the truly criminal. Sima Qian reports that in 115, young wastrels from wealthy families arrested for their gambling activities were able to purchase official pardons, and that after paying fines, a number of the young offenders were actually given posts as palace "gentlemen." A proverb about capital punishment that was popular during this time summarizes the situation well: "The lad with a thousand pounds of gold in place / Will not part with his head in the marketplace." The Han histories thus suggest that upper-class boys not only evaded being punished for their bad behavior but were at times virtually rewarded for it. Han historians also indicate that a number of aristocratic parents habitually indulged their children until they had committed crimes of such seriousness that no bribe or special plea could redeem them.

One such account concerns Princess Longlu (*Lowng-loo*), a younger sister of Emperor Wu, who calmed fears about her son's behavior by pre-purchasing a commutation of the death sentence in anticipation of his committing a serious crime. Unfortunately, after the princess died, her son murdered his wife's lady-in-waiting. Though it was Emperor Wu who had originally granted the commutation, when the case was tried, the emperor claimed he could not bring himself to tamper with the laws of his ancestors and had his nephew executed.

SCHOLARS AND OFFICIALS

The educated elite consisted of scholars and officials. Strictly speaking, scholars were highly educated men who engaged in teaching and research, who did not necessarily fill an official position in the government.

Their knowledge of classical texts earned them the highest status of all non-aristocratic groups. Officials were literate men who, though educated, worked as government administrators. A large centralized empire required the services of a sizable corps of literate officials, and one of the ways the Han strove to supply the demand for well-trained officials was through the establishment of a system of schools throughout the empire.

The Han is the first dynasty that has left behind clear historical evidence about educational institutions established by the central government for the instruction of the common people. The history of higher education in Han times is well documented. In the *Shiji*, Sima Qian sketched a brief outline of Han educational policy starting with the reign of Liu Bang:

> The emperor sighed over the neglected state of learning and would have done more to encourage its revival, but at the time there was still considerable turmoil within the empire. . . . Likewise, during the reigns of Emperor Hui and Empress Lü there was still no leisure to attend to the matter of government schools. Moreover, the high officials at the time were all military men who had won their distinction in battle. With the accession of Emperor Wen, Confucian scholars began little by little to be summoned and employed in government, although Emperor Wen himself rather favored the Legalist teachings on personnel organization and control.[3]

In 136, during the reign of Emperor Wu, the Five Confucian Classics achieved canonical status as the orthodox subject matter for state-sponsored study. With a curriculum consisting of the *Book of Documents*, the *Book of Songs*, the *Record of Ritual*, the *Classic of Changes*, and the *Spring and Autumn Annals*, Emperor Wu established the Imperial Academy in 124, which by the end of the Han dynasty (220 C.E.) enrolled more than thirty thousand students. Throughout the Han, boys between the ages of fourteen and seventeen attended the Imperial Academy. Later in the dynasty, there was a plan for the establishment of schools in all villages, though the extent to which the plan was ever realized remains unclear. As Hans Bielenstein has noted, education during this period still remained a luxury.

Han sources imply that, generally speaking, male children at age seven were thought to be ready to begin acquiring basic skills in reading, writing, and calculation. In an earlier day, according to the *Record of Rit-*

ual, boys learned arts associated with ritual (i.e., music and dance) at age twelve, and archery and chariot driving a little later. But by Han times, these militaristic accomplishments had already disappeared or were beginning to vanish from the curriculum. The same book suggests that girls concentrated on cultivating their knowledge of ritual, correct deportment, sericulture (silk production), and weaving.

The emphasis on education derived in part from the practical necessity of educating large numbers of youths who would eventually staff an increasingly complex bureaucracy. But it also paved the way for poor but determined boys to rise to positions of national importance. The young Ni Kuan (*Nee Kwan*; c. 120), for example, who hired himself out as a manual laborer to pay for his education and who "carried a copy of the classics with him as he hoed," eventually rose to the status of imperial counselor. Thus, according to Han Confucian thought, a boy's future social worth depended not on pedigree alone but on the gradual accumulation of virtue and learning as well. And though family wealth must have frequently determined a boy's access to education, the path to privilege, at least in theory, was open to all boys who could match Ni Kuan's perseverance.

One can hardly begin to appreciate the full significance of this idea in Han China until one recalls the relative newness of the belief that great men are made, not born. The idea that social and political privilege should be based on merit rather than pedigree first finds clear expression in Zhou dynasty documents. Confucius, as presented in the *Analects*, for example, "was not ashamed to ask and learn of his inferiors," and he insisted that "in teaching, there should be no distinction of classes."[4] Confucius recognized human worth or potential without regard for age, rank, and social background, especially in cases where others would be blinded by such external considerations. In the Warring States Era, the Chinese began to experience the practical application and actual effects of this belief in the sphere of statecraft and in patterns of social mobility. But it was not until the establishment of the Five Confucian Classics and the expansion of the civil service in the Han Empire that China witnessed the large-scale institutionalization of a merit-based system of advancement and privilege, at least in theory, for any man educated in the classics. Aristocratic families would continue to rise and fall throughout the Han, but for the less well-born, social prestige could now be acquired with growing regularity through intellectual and moral achievement.

Nonetheless, the sheer number of Han intellectuals who argumentatively stressed the necessity of study and the relative unimportance of pedigree attests to the fact that social and political privilege was still strongly associated with lineage rather than individual merit or achievement.

The ambivalent attitude toward aristocratic entitlement was largely due to Confucian beliefs that supported the granting of political power and privilege based on merit for officials, but still sanctioned the idea of a hereditary aristocracy for emperors and kings. In general, Han Confucians never sought to eliminate the emperor in their visions of ideal government. To the contrary, the elevation of Confucian scholars in Han society was at least partially the result of their defense and justification of the legitimacy of the ruling house. Han Confucian notions of a princely education designed to make the ruler a moral exemplar worthy of his position thus served to mediate between the conflicting notions that privilege is based on merit on the one hand, and on aristocratic birth on the other. In this way, Han Confucians were able to support imperial power while maintaining the ideal of the meritocracy.

FARMERS, MERCHANTS, ARTISANS, AND OTHER PROFESSIONALS

In the late Spring and Autumn Era, warfare waged in chariots by urban aristocrats increasingly gave way to battles between armies of foot soldiers recruited from the whole of the male rural population. With the reforms of Qin in about 359, the government "achieved the total identity of civil administration and military organization toward which earlier reforms had tended and which became the ideal of Legalist administrative theory."[5] The strength of the state rested on war and agriculture, which Legalist thinkers defined as the only occupations appropriate to the common people. Efficient and practical, the Qin state used resources that earlier rulers had ignored or could not find the wherewithal to marshal. The male peasantry could be made to work previously uncultivated land, pay taxes as household heads, perform conscript labor services, and extend the empire through military conquest. Military accomplishments among the common people were rewarded with elevation in the system of aristocratic ranks. Occasionally the state tried to encourage migration to underpopulated areas by awarding farmers who opened previously uncultivated areas with ranks and small parcels of land.

Peasant farmers included those who worked small plots of land that they owned, as well as tenants who rented and worked land held by others, landholders who did not till the land themselves but whose primary occupation involved managing farms, and finally hired farmhands who were paid to work the land owned by others. Although the state held farmers in high esteem because of the crucial nature of their efforts, farmers were generally poor and looked down on by elite members of society. Merchants, on the other hand, were despised by scholars and government officials alike because they were viewed as making no positive contribution to society but simply enriching themselves by circulating goods produced by others. Apart from a brief period during the reign of Emperor Wu, merchants were barred from officialdom, subject to strict sumptuary laws that restricted what they could wear and own, and taxed at a double rate. Artisans, while generally less able to enrich themselves, enjoyed a status below that of peasants but above that of merchants. Other professionals worked as physicians, veterinarians, butchers, and occultists (specialists who performed magical and religious rites, divined the future, and determined lucky days for various activities). The ideal social order is sometimes referred to with the catchy acronym SPAM: scholars on top, then peasants, artisans, and merchants.

ORDINARY WOMEN

In addition to utilizing the male peasantry, the Qin state understood the value of women's contributions to its power and wealth (see Figure 16). Ordinary women were occasionally made to participate in military operations but more typically they contributed to the state through the production of cloth. The importance of textile manufacture is clear in a society where cloth could be used in place of cash to pay fines and taxes, or where family members of those who produced large amounts of cloth were excused from conscript labor duty. As in earlier times, in the first years of the Han, the state utilized the female population's reproductive, military, and labor potential. Thus in 204 Liu Bang dressed some two thousand women in armor to trick the forces of Xiang Yu; in 200 Liu ordered that new parents be excused from labor service for two years; in 190 Emperor Hui decreed that families would have to pay five times the normal poll tax for unmarried girls age fifteen and older; in 191 he conscripted 145,000 female and male subjects to help build the city wall of the capital, Chang'an; and in 167 Empress Dou personally raised silk worms to produce cloth in order to encourage all women of the empire to engage in sericulture.

Imperial edicts in the next two reigns indicate a shift away from the Qin-inspired utilization of the female population. The reigns of Emperors Wen and Jing, the former in particular, are notable not so much for the labor services women provided to the state but for the many charitable acts by imperial decree that benefited the general female population. For example, in 180, on the day of Emperor Wen's coronation, the male head of each household was granted one step in noble rank while the women were presented with oxen and wine for feasting.

A new feature of rulership introduced by the Qin state was that power now extended directly from the throne to each individual member of the population. In addition to functioning as a means to collect taxes and conscript military and labor services, the direct relationship between the ruler and the common people helped establish a social order among people without blood relationships who were resettled in areas recently conquered or newly opened for cultivation. But this form of imperial domination functioned effectively only when the people accepted that rule as legitimate. The Han emperors were quite aware of the need to ensure the loyalty of their subjects, and to that end, they made periodic dispensations to them in the form of amnesties, ranks, and feasts. They presented gifts of meat and wine to all women in the empire, most often at the same time that ranks were bestowed on the men to celebrate, for example, the enthronement of a new emperor, the naming of an heir apparent or empress, or the change of a reign title. The effort to include women in these grants demonstrates the importance the empire attached to winning the allegiance (and productivity) of its female populace. The large-scale and complex activities and agenda of the centralized state required the ruler to take stock of, utilize, and develop the potential of his human resources to the fullest.

MARRIAGE AND SUCCESSION PRACTICES

Historical sources do not provide much information about ordinary marriages (other than the fact that they seemed to have been arranged by the parents), but the historical records do provide details about the marriage practices of the aristocracy. A major change in the early years of the Han Empire was that the rules by which Han emperors appointed empresses and heirs apparent were more flexible than they had been in previous eras. In the Spring and Autumn Era, for example, a ruler's principal bride was accompanied by sisters or nieces, who simultaneously became secondary wives. In this way, if the principal wife died or proved barren, the political alliance between the ruler's state and the wife's state continued to be upheld by the wife's close kin—women who shared her loyalties to her natal state and family. Though the system could be manipulated, it did not have the flexibility of the Han system, in which the emperor could replace a deceased or barren empress with almost any girl or woman in his harem who captured his affections. Texts that recount the history of the Spring and Autumn Era document instances of barren consorts who possessed enough favor and clout to appropriate or adopt the son of a concubine, yet this option was not generally exercised in the Han. When maintaining interstate alliances was no longer a consideration, the emphasis shifted from retaining a barren consort (in the interests of her family and state) to elevating to empress whoever was the mother of the heir apparent.

For example, Emperor Wu's first empress, Empress Chen (*Chun*), paid $90 billion cash—a phenomenal amount of money—to doctors to help her conceive a boy. When she failed to produce a son, there were no sympathetic sisters or cousins to assume her reproductive duties and protect her interests. She was deposed, and a former slave, Wei Zifu (*Way Dzuh-foo*), who gave birth to Emperor Wu's first son, took her place. Similarly, Emperor Wen's queen died before he became emperor, and all of her sons died in infancy. When Wen ascended the imperial throne, because his concubine Lady Dou was the mother of his eldest son, that boy was made heir apparent, and his mother was consequently made empress. Thus, like Wei Zifu, Lady Dou received her rank through her son.

The woman who produced a son and possessed the affections of the emperor was thus in the strongest position to be named empress and have her son appointed heir apparent. Ultimately, her social status, her family connections, and the birth order of her son mattered little, since a determined emperor could depose or—if he was sufficiently ruthless—simply have executed any inconvenient empresses and heirs who had fallen from favor. Occasionally, however, powerful groups at court could exert enough pressure to override the emperor's preference. Though primogeniture became the established norm (though not necessarily the actual practice) in

Han times, the lack of established procedures and precedents at the out-set of the dynasty allowed for a certain degree of imperial capriciousness and generated the factional strife that was often the consequence of leav-ing the position of heir apparent and empress open to many contenders. Combined with the autocratic tendencies of certain emperors, the highly flexible system also failed to protect the incumbents after they had been selected—Wei Zifu herself fell from favor and died by her own hand in 91. Nonetheless, these conditions, dangerous as they were, provided ample opportunities for clever girls to maneuver themselves into positions of honor despite their lowly social backgrounds.

Gaining entry into the inner circles of the court allowed a girl to bring honors to her family as well, due to other political developments of the Han, which created new, informal opportunities for women. We have al-ready seen how the kingdoms first given to the emperor's paternal kins-men were eventually stripped away after it became clear that the members of the Liu imperial family could not be trusted with large territories and independent authority. By 145 kings were no longer permitted to rule over their domains. Emperor Wu later dealt the final blow when he decreed that kings could no longer bequeath their kingdoms to a single heir but had to divide up their territories equally among all their sons.

These policies emptied the imperial court of the emperor's paternal kinsmen and weakened them politically by enfeoffing them (i.e., award-ing them) with small territories away from the capital over which they had little or no official authority. While the goal of these policies was to rid the emperor of the threat of rebel kinsmen, an unintended result was that they created a power vacuum at court. Exacerbating this sudden shift in the balance of power was Emperor Wu's decision to take the initiative in ruling and override the authority of his chancellors. The chancellor was the official to whom previous Han rulers had delegated their pow-ers. He was also the official who made criticism of the government al-lowable in a way that was impossible after government policy began to flow directly from the emperor. The emperor also increasingly conducted business within the confines of his harem, a place that was shut off to all other males except his eunuchs. The members of the imperial consort families gladly filled the ensuing power vacuum, serving as the emperor's chief allies and buffers against antagonistic power holders in the bureau-cracy. Under these conditions, a daughter like Wei Zifu was in a stronger position to better the fortunes of her family than a boy of the same social background: only a daughter could marry an emperor, give birth to his heir, and—as the mother of an underage son—rule the empire as empress dowager after her imperial husband's death.

Indeed, once Wei Zifu was appointed empress, Wei Qing (*Way Cheeng*) and Huo Qubing (*Whoa Chew-beeng*), her brother and nephew, respectively, became two of the dynasty's most celebrated generals; Huo Guang (*Whoa Gwang*), her sister's stepson (half-brother of Huo Qubing), came to occupy the office of marshal of state, one of the most powerful positions in the government; her son was named imperial heir apparent; and her great-grandson acceded to the throne as Emperor Xuan (*Shwuen*; r. 74–49 B.C.E.). Women who occupied key positions in the imperial family—such as the empress, the emperor's mother (empress dowager), and the emperor's sisters and daughters (princesses)—were all given landed estates and incomes, fiefs that they were entitled to transmit to their sons.

Although early Han emperors were not compelled to select their spouses in order to stabilize interstate politics, as Jennifer Holmgren has pointed out, many still had little say in the selection of a first wife. They were often married at an early age to women—or girls—chosen by their mothers, grandmothers, or aunts. Holmgren has also rightly observed that because rulers did not always get along with the empresses forced on them by the older generation, the concubines the emperors chose for themselves were more likely to be favored and produce heirs to the throne. For example, Empress Chen, Emperor Wu's first consort, was the daughter of his paternal aunt and the granddaughter of the formidable Grand Empress Dowager Dou. According to the wishes of Princess Liu Piao (*Leo Pee-ow*; she was Emperor Jing's sister and Emperor Wu's aunt), Empress Chen had been married to Emperor Wu when he became heir apparent in 150, that is, when he was little more than six years old. The *Han shu* says that despite her not having produced any sons, Empress Chen was arrogant and made much of her powerful connections at court, frequently reminding Emperor Wu that he had come to the throne because of her mother's (Princess Liu Piao's) efforts. With the death of the grand empress dowager in 135, Empress Chen lost a powerful ally. Finally, in 128, when Wei Zifu gave birth to Emperor Wu's first son, Empress Chen was deposed on the grounds of using witchcraft to win back the emperor's affections (a charge for which her daughter suffered execution).

Holmgren also notes that imperial kinswomen and particularly princesses, in contrast to most men of the Liu imperial family, often resided near the center of power, where they were able to entertain the emperor at their own courts and, as women, enjoy access to the inner court of the imperial palace. Furthermore, unlike the emperor's brothers who were viewed as possible contenders to the throne, the emperor could be fairly certain of his sisters' loyalties, since their fortunes rested on their brother's secure grasp on power. Imperial princesses were therefore ideally positioned to introduce women to the emperor. Moreover, unlike an aunt, mother, or grandmother, a sister of the emperor was probably less likely to try to impose her will on the ruler and more apt to let him choose a woman or girl according to his own wishes and desires.

GIRLS

For elite and humble women alike, it is important to point out that a girl's marriage was regarded as an issue of crucial importance from the moment of her birth. First of all, a family's decision to raise or dispose of a female infant was often determined by its assessment of her prospects for making a good marriage and how large a dowry the family might be required to pay. An optimistic view of a girl's future therefore positively affected not only her reception at birth but also the kind of training and education she would receive. Second of all, in Han times, most girls married between the ages of thirteen and sixteen, and probably many of them before they reached their majority—age fifteen, the point at which the Han government demanded the adult poll tax. Thus in early China, marriage as either wife or concubine shaped the nature of and often occurred within a girl's childhood.

The *Taiping jing*—a text that probably dates from Han times and that has been described as "a thesaurus of religious ideas current among the commoners of China"—contains one of the most explicit statements on the frequency with which infants were killed or exposed: "Now under Heaven, all families kill girls; and under Heaven, how many hundreds of thousands of families are there? There are even some families that have killed more than ten girls."[6] The text is unique in early China in that it specifically condemns killing, or "disposing of," female infants. Boys were traditionally valued more than girls because girls always married into their husband's family line. That is, any effort and expense that went into raising a daughter was a loss because when she married, she would move in with her husband's family, take care of his parents in their old age, and worship his ancestors with the offerings needed to nourish their spirits. After marriage, contact with her birth family could be limited, and any couple that produced only daughters might eventually find themselves impoverished and alone—in this world and the next.

This sort of thinking led to the perception of female infants as extraneous elements weakening the prosperity of their natal families, which in turn justified killing them at birth. The benefits of practicing female infanticide are illustrated in a statement attributed to the Legalist philosopher Han Feizi (*Hahn Fey-dzuh*; d. 233), who appears to be commenting on attitudes prevalent in his day: "Parents' attitudes toward children are such that . . . they congratulate each other when it is a boy and kill it if it is a girl because they are considering their later convenience and calculating their long-term interests."[7] It is nevertheless clear that female infants were not universally despised as mere drains on family resources, and especially in Han times, conditions arose that made families reassess a daughter's ability to improve the lot of her family.

Unlike commoner boys, whose most efficient route to high governmental positions lay in acquiring military or administrative skills, low-status freeborn girls gained entry into government service by occupying the only positions available to them: palace servants, entertainers, and concubines. A concubine's status in society was not necessarily low. By the first century B.C.E., imperial concubines had been graded into fourteen different ranks that corresponded to the bureaucratic positions that men occupied. Thus, a "brilliant companion" was equivalent to a chancellor, and she received the same income he did.

Between 141 and 48 B.C.E., the demand for girls who were willing to enter the harems of the wealthy and noble soared. This trend is documented in a memorial by Gong Yu (*Gohng You*; d. 44) complaining about the excessive numbers of women serving as imperial concubines, in which he noted that from the reign of Emperor Liu Bang to that of Emperor Jing, the imperial harem included no more than twelve women at a time. Small wonder that he should criticize the emperor, for according to the *Han shu*, after the reigns of Emperors Wu and Yuan, the figure jumped to an astounding three thousand. Moreover, that number did not include the concubines of the heir apparent, kings, or marquises. Kings, according to Gong Yu, typically owned several hundred concubines. Around 81, a Confucian critic complained that even high officials and wealthy men of the day kept scores of women in their households, and pointed out that because the wealthy and noble continued to amass such large harems, many ordinary men had to remain unmarried.

The instances of girls who joined the imperial harem and ended up as empresses are few. Ambitious parents who entered a daughter into service at the imperial court could only hope that the girl would distinguish herself from the multitude of others like her, find favor with the emperor, and produce a son. But even the family of a less spectacularly fortunate concubine could probably expect to see some share of its daughter's income. In surroundings of such wealth and luxury, even a lowly serving girl might occasionally receive tips, bribes, or gifts to pass on to her family. There were other benefits as well. For example, after Emperor Jing died, his testamentary edict freed all of the women in his harem and exempted them from taxation for the remainder of their lives. (For an unusual example of how an educated girl from a prominent family appealed directly to the emperor on her father's behalf, see Document 11.)

SLAVES

Slaves were never as numerous or as important to the economy in China as they were in the Roman Empire, but there were slaves in early China, and they made up perhaps one percent of a total population of around 50 million people. According to the law of collective responsibility, family members of criminals guilty of certain crimes were made government (as opposed to private) slaves; commoners could also be sold into slavery if they or their family could not pay off debts. Some slaves were presented as gifts to the government; others were confiscated from their owners as punishment for various kinds of illegal activities; and still others, though a small minority, were Chinese as well as non-Chinese prisoners of war. Both government and private slave status were hereditary, but slaves could purchase their freedom or have it granted by their owners. A large number of the government's female slaves served in the imperial palace.

In addition to maintaining slaves for their own use, emperors gave members of the imperial family and meritorious or favored individuals slaves, some of whom appear to have become private property after bestowal. Wealthy people also bought peasants who had been sold into slavery or had otherwise come on the slave market, a practice that appears to have been commonplace even though the sale of free individuals was deemed illegal in Han times under most circumstances. Motivated by profit or economic duress, peasants frequently sold their children. Parents whose daughters had been trained in special skills could command high prices for their offspring. Around 160, for example, the king of Jibei purchased four girls who were skilled acrobats for more than $4 billion in cash. By all accounts, this was an extraordinarily high price, the standard being between $12,000 and $20,000 in cash. Han sources tell us that free individuals could also be kidnapped and put up for sale on the slave market.

Ties between elites and their slaves in the early Han could operate as a potent force that bypassed both kinship structures and official bureaucratic channels. In this period, the collaboration between elites and slaves, an alliance that sometimes brought benefits to both parties, emerges with increasing frequency. It is well known that in early Han times aristocrats and landowners who lacked official authority still frequently controlled local political affairs and used unlawful means to demand labor, tribute, and other services from the people. They achieved such ends by employing male slaves as spies, strongmen, and private armed militia to terrorize the local populace, threaten officials, and obstruct justice.

In a period marked by increasing slave ownership, high-ranking women also joined forces with their female slaves to form partnerships that extended the authority of both parties involved. The relationship between a servant named Miss Tang (*Tahng*) and Lady Cheng (*Chung*), one of Emperor Jing's concubines, reveals the very intimate sphere in which slave-elite cooperation could operate. On one occasion, Emperor Jing summoned Lady Cheng to his bedchamber, but because it was her "time of the month," Lady Cheng dressed the maid in her own clothes and sent her to the emperor instead. The emperor was drunk and favored the serving girl without realizing she was not Lady Cheng. Somewhat later, when Emperor Jing discovered that the serving girl had given birth to a son as a result of this meeting, he named the boy Fa (Discovery) and appointed him king of Changsha.

But the histories also suggest that aristocratic women used slaves in ways that benefited the slave mistress alone. The *Han shu* notes several cases in which elite women ordered their female slaves to commit crimes. For example, sometime around 125, a concubine of the king of Hengshan named Xulai (*Shoe-lie*) secretly commanded a female slave to poison the king's consort. After this was accomplished, Xulai was made queen. She then ordered one of the king's female slaves to seduce the king's (not her own) son, Prince Xiao (Sha-ow), in order to incriminate the prince and move her own son into position to be named heir to the throne. As a result, Prince Xiao was executed in the marketplace for the crime of incest, since having sexual relations with a woman favored by one's father was strictly taboo.

Han law punished slaves for reporting the crimes of their masters (according to the same legal principle that prevented children from informing on their parents). The slave girls forced to commit these deeds were thus powerless to report them or to seek the help of the authorities. Moreover, the newly excavated Zhangjiashan (Johng-jee-aw-shawn; in Hubei province) legal code states that a slave owner could ask the government to punish a disobedient slave with death. But according to legal texts, the government went to some pains to investigate cases concerning disobedient slaves. A slave owner would therefore have had no interest in reporting a slave for not carrying out an illegal order, especially since Han historical texts suggest that slave owners who ordered their slaves to commit certain crimes, such as murder, were punished for the same crime when the case was substantiated by official inquiries. For example, in the course of investigating a case of treason, the crimes of Queen Xulai came to light, and she was executed for her role in the poisoning of her predecessor, though the murder had actually been committed by her slave. It is not known how slaves fared in these cases.

Slave girls were also occasionally subjected to sadistic abuse. One particularly shocking case involved King Jian (Jen) of Jiangdu (c. 122), who punished female slaves by throwing them to wolves because he found it amusing to watch them being eaten alive. Rumors about how slaves and serving girls suffered at the hands of their superiors must have circulated as freely among the common people as news concerning the astonishing wealth and favor enjoyed by the few who rose from poverty to privilege. The common people were therefore most likely well aware of slavery's risks as well as its benefits.

THE FAMILY

The *Shiji* tells us that sometime around 359 in the state of Qin, Shang Yang established a law requiring "persons with two or more adult sons and not living separately . . . to pay a double tax." And then somewhat later, a law was established prohibiting fathers and adult sons, and older and younger brothers, from living in the same house. The Qin's legal requirement that adult sons establish separate residences (and thus separate families) was probably intended to expand the amount of cultivated land and the tax base, as well as to break the strength of large clans. One scholar also notes that "the reorganization of the family into small units also made the children more independent. Such statesmen as Jia Yi condemned the new attitudes of individualism, which differed so blatantly from those principles of filial piety that had dominated the previous period."[8] But filial piety, or reverence for and obedience to parents, continued to play a strong role in the Han family.

Throughout the Han, the concept of filial piety was primarily associated with the duties and attitudes of adult offspring toward their parents. This is not to say that young children were not expected to obey and revere their parents. Children were clearly taught about filial piety, but they were normally not in a position to practice it. What was emphasized was that offspring should cheerfully provide financial support to aged parents, produce offspring to carry on ancestral sacrifices, and preserve and bring honors (through public recognition) to the good name of the family— duties small children normally could not perform.

The authority traditionally granted to parents over their children, which was partially supported by the state, worked in tandem with the religious and cultural ideal of filial piety to ensure that children would care for their aging parents. But in negative terms, these traditions also bolstered the autocratic power of elders over juniors and contributed to the victimization of imperial and ordinary children alike. Nevertheless, from Warring States times onward, China witnessed an increasing effort in both the legal and the religious sphere to limit the autocratic power of parents over their offspring. Under Qin law, a father who wanted to punish a child with death was required to go through the agency of the state—not to request permission to punish the child himself, but to have the state carry out the punishment.

In Qin and Han times, it was illegal (and usually punishable by tattooing and hard labor) for a parent to kill his or her own child. Though the Han legal code excavated in 1983 at Zhangjiashan is incomplete, it does tell us that a parent who administered a beating that unintentionally resulted in the child's death was subject to the redeemable death penalty (i.e., he was required to pay a fine in lieu of the punishment). The punishment for the premeditated murder of offspring was undoubtedly more severe. That the state interposed itself between the parent's wrath and the offending child supplied at least a limited safeguard against a parent taking his child's life in the heat of the moment. Further, the state did not rely on the parent's accusation but required independent verification that the crime had been committed. At the same time, according to Qin and early Han law, children and slaves were not entitled to bring—and in fact were punished for bringing—official accusations against their parents or masters.

The legal texts excavated at Zhangjiashan show that mothers also possessed the power to request that family dependents be punished by death. One case, for example, concerns a widow whose mother-in-law reported her to the authorities for committing adultery behind her recently deceased husband's coffin. Presiding officials discussed prosecuting her for unfiliality—the punishment for which was execution followed by the exposure of one's corpse in the marketplace—though the offending daughter-in-law's life was finally spared after much discussion and disagreement. This case illustrates that a mother as well as a father could hand an offending child over to the authorities, who, if upon investigating the case found the allegations true, would put the child to death. Indeed, the *Han shu* records a story about a woman whose stepson was punished with death after she reported him to the authorities for unfilial behavior.

It is only fair to point out, however, that these cases concern adult offspring and not young children. According to the recently excavated Han laws, children below age ten were exempt from all punishments apart from cases of homicide or rebellion, and those below seventeen were exempt from mutilating punishments. Nevertheless, the mere existence of laws that allowed parents to ask to have unfilial adult offspring put to death, and that prohibited offspring of any age from making accusations against their parents, must have contributed to a child's sense that disobedience was simply not an option. Scholars characterize the Han family as a hierarchically structured political and religious unit, with male elders in positions of authority over women and younger members, but with all members under the watchful eyes of the emperor in this world, and deceased ancestors in the world beyond.

APPENDIX: THE TWENTY HAN ORDERS OF ARISTOCRATIC RANK

1. Gongshi: Gentleman

2. Shangzao: Distinguished Accomplishment

3. Zanniao: Ornamented Horses

4. Bugeng: No Conscript Service

5. Dafu: Grandee

6. Guan Dafu: Government Grandee

7. Gong Dafu: Gentleman Grandee

8. Gongcheng: Gentleman Chariot

9. Wu Dafu: Grandee

10. Zuo Shuzhang: Chief of the Multitude on the Left

11. You Shuzhang: Chief of the Multitude on the Right

12. Zuo Geng: Chieftain of Conscripts on the Left

13. Zhong Geng: Chieftain of Conscripts in the Center

14. You Geng: Chieftain of Conscripts on the Right

15. Shao Shangzao: Second-Order Distinguished Accomplishment

16. Da Shangzao: Most Distinguished Accomplishment

17. Siju Shuzhang: Chieftain of the Multitude Riding a Four-Horse Chariot

18. Da Shuzhang: Grand Chieftain of the Multitude

19. Guannei Hou: Marquis of the Imperial Domain

20. Che Hou: Full Marquis[9]

NOTES

1. *Analects*, 2.10; Arthur Waley, trans., *The Analects of Confucius* (New York: Vintage Books, 1938), p. 90.

2. Burton Watson, trans., *Records of the Grand Historian, Han Dynasty*, 2 vols., rev. ed. (New York and Hong Kong: *Renditions*-Columbia University Press, 1993), 1:395, 2:329.

3. Watson's trans., *Han*, 2:357.

4. *Analects*, 5.14 and 15.38; James Legge, trans., *Confucian Analects, the Great Learning, and the Doctrine of the Mean* (Oxford: Clarendon Press, 1893).

5. Mark Edward Lewis, *Sanctioned Violence in Early China* (Albany: State University of New York Press, 1990), p. 62.

6. Max Kaltenmark, "The Ideology of the T'ai-p'ing ching," in *Facets of Taoism: Essays in Chinese Religion*, ed. Holmes Welch and Anna Seidel (New Haven: Yale University Press, 1979), p. 38.

7. Translated by Bernice J. Lee, "Female Infanticide in China," in *Women in China: Current Directions in Historical Scholarship*, ed. Richard W. Guisso and Stanley Johannesen (Youngstown, NY: Philo Press, 1981), p. 164.

8. Ch'ü T'ung-tsu, *Han Social Structure* (Seattle: University of Washington Press, 1972), p. 253, n. 9.

9. Translations of titles based on Rafe de Crespigny, *Official Titles of the Former Han Dynasty* (Canberra: Australian National University Press, 1967).

CHAPTER 5

IMPERIAL CHINA IN WORLD HISTORY

It took about a century from the founding of the Han Empire in 202 B.C.E. until the high point of Emperor Wu's reign in 104 B.C.E. to put the dynasty and the empire on a solid foundation. China was by that time politically and culturally unified under a centrally administered government, the imperial sponsorship of the Five Confucian Classics confirmed Confucian learning as a basis for state ideology, and bureaucrats whose positions depended on their performance in office held power. Although Emperor Wu's military ambitions would strain the financial resources of the empire, agricultural productivity had advanced far beyond what it had been in previous centuries, and China was a relatively prosperous nation. A dynamic balance had been worked out between the inner court, members of the imperial clan, civil administrators, and the military. Local elite families, merchants, and peasants all played crucial—though restricted—roles in society, and the Chinese had developed methods to ensure their security amid the nomadic neighboring peoples that surrounded them.

Even though this system of government was fairly stable by the standards of the ancient world, the challenges of keeping an empire together were enormous. There was a brief dynastic crisis in 9 C.E. when Wang Mang, the father of the reigning empress (and not a member of the Liu imperial family), seized power and claimed that he would bring Confucian solutions to the problem of the increasing power of wealthy families and their huge estates. He was killed in 25 C.E. by a coalition of such families, who then restored a member of the Liu clan to the throne. The Han Empire continued for another two centuries before conflict among consort families, eunuchs, and peasant rebels resulted in open warfare that divided the empire into three kingdoms and brought the Han to an end.

By 220 c.e. the Han dynasty was officially over, but it was not forgotten. Over the next three-and-a-half centuries, many generals who controlled an army and some land hastened to claim the Mandate of Heaven and call themselves emperor. Yet no one was able to unify all of China, and at any given time, there were several leaders who founded competing dynasties and insisted that their followers address them as "emperor." In many ways, this situation was similar to what would happen in Europe three centuries later after the fall of the Roman Empire in 476 c.e. Justinian, Charlemagne, and others tried to reunify the empire, but these efforts all failed. (See the Greenwood Guides to Historic Events of the Ancient World volume on the emperor Justinian.) Even when a powerful leader regained substantial territory, his family lost control of it within a generation or so. The dream of European unification lived on even into the twentieth century, but despite the best efforts of kings and statesmen, Rome was gone forever. Today Europe comprises more than thirty different nations, and the North African and Middle Eastern lands once governed by the Romans are similarly divided among several modern countries.

Somewhat amazingly, however, China was unified again in the sixth century by the Sui dynasty (589–618). And with the brief exception of the Five Dynasties Era (907–960), China was never again thrown into complete political chaos. Certainly there was the dynastic cycle, with different families gaining and then losing power, but the Chinese managed to discover an extraordinarily successful mode of political and social organization. As far as they knew, there was only one way to organize a nation. Indeed, despite some limited contacts with India, the Chinese thought of themselves as the only civilized people in the world; the choice was either the Chinese way or the "barbarian" way, that is, the lifestyles of nomadic and illiterate peoples to the west, south, and north.

It is true that China was sometimes taken over by nomadic invaders— apparently the Chinese emphasis on civilized arts often left them weak on defense—but Chinese culture demonstrated a remarkable ability to absorb barbarian conquerors. Usually the new overseers settled down and became Sinicized ("Chinese-ified"). That is, they began to eat Chinese food, wear Chinese clothes, marry Chinese women, and speak Chinese. Over the course of several generations, they became indistinguishable from native-born Chinese. In time, new barbarian peoples would appear on the borders to begin the process again. Even the Mongols—perhaps the fiercest of the nomadic warriors—fit this pattern to some degree. Genghis Khan's original plan for China in the thirteenth century was to burn all the cities, kill all the people, and turn the empire into pasture-land for his horses. He had a Chinese adviser—himself from assimilated nomadic ancestry—who recommended instead that the Mongols keep the basic Chinese system of government intact. In this way the Chinese would continue to pay taxes, and the Mongols could enjoy all the benefits. This was indeed the course the Mongols followed, with Genghis' grandson, Khubilai Khan, setting up a Chinese-style dynasty called the Yuan (1264–1368) and appointing himself emperor.

The Yuan dynasty was followed by the Ming (1368–1644), a native Chinese dynasty, which eventually gave way to the Qing (1644–1911), another conquest regime. In this last instance, the nomads were Manchus from the northeast of China, and from the beginning they set out to show that they were more committed to Chinese traditions than were the Ming emperors they had replaced. Although a few westerners like Marco Polo had traveled to China during the time of the Mongols, it was during the Qing dynasty that Europeans representing modernized, aggressive nation-states began to arrive in considerable numbers. Some of the first were Jesuit missionaries like Matteo Ricci (1552–1610). These men were extremely well-educated and versatile, and since they had arrived in an era of Chinese power and prosperity, they sent back glowing reports to their superiors in Europe. They recognized many of the strengths of Chinese culture and became experts in Chinese literature and philosophy. In the nineteenth century, however, when many more Western traders and Protestant missionaries arrived, China was undergoing significant financial and political turmoil. By that time Europe had become even more militarily and economically dominant in world affairs, and the long-standing pattern of Chinese-foreigner relations was disrupted. Westerners viewed China as backwards and ignorant, and even to many Chinese observers it appeared that the traditions of imperial China were a hindrance to modernization. The last Chinese emperor abdicated his throne on February 12, 1912, bringing to an end over 2,100 years of imperial rule.

Many Westerners assumed that the China they encountered in the nineteenth century was substantially the same as it had always been. This

wasn't true; over the previous two thousand years there had been enormous changes, including the introduction of Buddhism, shifts in taxation
and the distribution of land, modifications in gender roles and family relations, industrialization, and commercial expansion. However, China
did exhibit a strong continuity with the past, and many of the oldest and
most esteemed characteristics of Chinese culture dated back to the beginning of the imperial era. The people and rulers of China thought of
themselves as continuing a way of life that had been developed in the
Han Empire.

THE LEGACY OF THE HAN EMPIRE IN EAST ASIA

Perhaps the most important inheritance from the Han was the ideal
of a stable, enduring, politically unified China, with power concentrated
at the center. Ever since the Qin and Han showed that this was possible, the Chinese have been uncomfortable with the idea of a divided
China. The long stretch of imperial history included several centuries of
intense civil war and times when foreign invaders controlled significant
portions of the country (conditions that prevailed during the first half of
the twentieth century as well), but the sense that Chinese civilization
required territorial and political unity has not diminished. Indeed, even
now, nearly a century after the last emperor, China is ruled by a political system in which power is focused on the central government in Beijing. This offers a striking contrast to Europe; although China has almost
twice the territory and well over twice the population of Europe, it is
today a single nation (with the exception of Taiwan, which is still a major
point of contention).

At a basic level, an empire is a political entity held together by military force, but to survive it needs the cooperation and support of both
the general populace and the ruling class. It has to seem in the interest
of many people to keep an empire going. After Lu Jia's famous comment
to Liu Bang that one could win an empire on horseback, but not rule it
on horseback, he elaborated, "To pay due attention to both civil and military affairs is the way for a dynasty to achieve long life. . . . If, after it
had united the world under its rule, Qin had practiced benevolence and
righteousness and modeled its ways upon the sages of antiquity, how
would Your Majesty ever have been able to win possession of the empire?"[1] It was control of both civil concerns (*wen*) and military affairs

(*wu*) that made the empire possible. The term *wen* refers not just to bureaucratic administration but also to the blessings of civilization, including art, ritual, literature, philosophy, and scholarship. Many of these
pursuits were, of course, out of reach for ordinary people, but the peasants nevertheless benefited from peace and civil order, and from a government that concerned itself with the welfare of the common people.
If empires had to be gained and maintained by force, they were worth
fighting for because they made possible a certain way of life. Confucian
philosophers had long taught that only the ruler who provides a stable
livelihood for the people—that is, one where freedom from hunger and
violence prevails—can go on to educate his people and usher them into
an era of enduring peace and high civilization. Imperial China was not
simply a creation of despots or military dictators; it spread its advantages
widely.

In addition to a conception of empire that made it seem a desirable
or even normal state of affairs, the following are some of the major in-
heritances that later imperial China derived from the Han:

Literature. The Han dynasty was a time when multitudes of scholars
worked to preserve and consolidate the remnants of ancient Chinese culture. What we know today of early Chinese philosophy and
history comes for the most part from the efforts of Han scholars.
The accepted versions of the Confucian Classics, our present texts
of Warring States philosophy, the historical accounts of the *Shiji*,
and the essays and poetry of Han writers formed the foundation for
Chinese literary culture. Even the style of writing was much admired in later centuries, and in the Tang dynasty (618–907), there
was a deliberate attempt to return to the elegance and simplicity of
Han models. As late as the Qing dynasty (1644–1911), a school of
"Han Learning" was prominent. Emperor Wu set a precedent for
the official sponsorship of Confucian scholarship, and in later dynasties, the government supported the writing of twenty-four more
"standard histories"—accounts of individual dynasties based on the
model of Sima Qian's *Shiji* and Ban Gu's *Han shu*.

Specific administrative techniques. These included the division of the
country into commanderies and counties; the organization of the
central government into civil, military, and censorate branches; the

writing of extensive law codes based on Qin and Han precedents; and the basic methods of handling taxes, reports, memorials (basic policy recommendations submitted by officials), and edicts (orders from the emperor). Other influential Han practices included military conscription based on population registers, as well as flexible relations with nomadic peoples that utilized warfare, diplomacy, trade, gifts, and intermarriage with Chinese princesses. Many of these administrative techniques had their origins in Qin legal practices, but the rule of law—in the sense that everyone, including the emperor, was subject to the same legal standards—never prevailed in China. Rather, there was rule *by* law; that is, emperors and other officials used the law to get the results they wanted.

Ideology. The Legalism inherent in the Han Empire was made palatable by the adoption of Confucianism as a state ideology. The emphasis on morality and humaneness in Confucius' ideas tempered the focus on power and efficiency that had characterized the Qin dynasty. In addition, Confucianism provided inspiration and an informal restraint on the actions of bureaucrats, who often owed their position to their mastery of the values taught by the Classics. Even though Buddhism gained popularity in the centuries that followed the Han, Confucianism nevertheless provided the primary mode of understanding human nature, social relations, government, and the natural world.

Ideas of sovereignty. Later Chinese emperors, like those in the Han, saw themselves as mediators between the human and the celestial realms, and they buttressed their authority by sponsoring official calendars that tracked the motions of the heavens. They owed their position, of course, to their ancestors, whom they honored with appropriate rituals, but they also recognized their own responsibility for maintaining order. They were the supreme exemplars of moral conduct, regarded as the "father and mother" of the common people. Moreover, since natural disasters might be Heaven's response to their personal shortcomings, they had to set an example of virtue, diligence, and respect for Heaven and the ancestors. While they oversaw the functions of government, they themselves were served by scores or even hundreds of eunuchs, concubines, musicians, and craftsmen.

Bureaucracy. Emperors may have ruled, but the real work of governing was carried out by thousands of salaried, professional administrators. Eventually there arose the ideal of the selfless bureaucrat—educated, loyal, and honest—who would risk death to speak out against abuse and corruption, even to his superiors. Needless to say, this lofty standard did not always match what happened in government offices around the empire, but it nevertheless exerted a powerful cultural influence. In later imperial China, officials were recruited through nationwide civil service exams, and the examiners went to great lengths to ensure that the competition was fair and open. Winners in the imperial exams were regarded as national heroes, and there was a surprising degree of social mobility as clever boys from less-advantaged backgrounds might hope that hard work would result in an official position—the most admirable of all possible careers. Once again, the beginnings of this system can be traced to the Han Empire, when Emperor Wen in 165 B.C.E. issued an edict ordering "the vassal kings, the ministers, and the commandery administrators to present to the Emperor those who were capable and good, and could speak frankly and admonish their superiors unflinchingly. The Emperor in person questioned them by setting a literary exercise."[2]

Just as later dynasties looked to the Han for inspiration and useful models, so did foreign countries. Vietnam, which had been taken over by the Han Empire in 111 B.C.E., gained its independence a thousand years later in the tenth century, but by that time its culture and government had absorbed much of Chinese civilization. It was ruled by an emperor who was served by bureaucrats chosen through an examination system based on the Confucian Classics. Though only the size of a Chinese commandery, it was subdivided into commanderies and counties. The educated elite adopted Chinese styles of literature, dress, and conduct despite the fact that the language, customs, and religion of the Vietnamese people were very different from the Chinese. The situation was similar in Korea, portions of which had been conquered by the Chinese under Emperor Wu. Korea had greater political independence from China than did Vietnam (direct Chinese rule on the peninsula did not last long), yet it too adopted Chinese models of government and philosophy. In particular, the Yi dynasty of Korea (1392–1910) adopted Confucianism as its official ideology, with all the social and political institutions associated with it.

Japan did not become a literate society until the seventh century, when the ruling class there adopted the Chinese script to represent their own language (not at all related to Chinese). Then began a wholesale, deliberate process of borrowing from China. Of course, they were borrowing from the contemporary Tang dynasty rather than the Han, but many of the ideas and practices that came across the China Sea were derived from earlier times. As in Vietnam and Korea, they adopted Chinese models, at the same time adapting them to their own needs. For example, though the Japanese spoke of the Mandate of Heaven, they managed to avoid the dynastic cycle—only one dynasty has ever ruled in Japan, down to the present emperor. And Japanese emperors could retire—unlike Chinese emperors, whose rule was only ended by death. There were no eunuchs in Japan, civil service exams were open only to aristocrats, and a real bureaucracy never developed. The situation of these border civilizations can be quickly summarized by chapter titles from the influential textbook *East Asia: Tradition and Transformation* by the Harvard scholars John K. Fairbank, Edwin O. Reischauer, and Albert M. Craig: "Vietnam: A Variant of the Chinese Pattern," "Early Korea: The Emergence of a Chinese Type of State," "Yi Dynasty Korea: A Model Confucian Society," "Early Japan: The Absorption of Chinese Civilization," and "Feudal Japan: A Departure from the Chinese Pattern."

HAN CHINA AND THE WIDER WORLD

At the time of the Han Empire, there was almost no contact between China and other advanced civilizations of the world. The Greeks and the Romans knew nothing of China, and the Chinese in turn had never heard of Homer and Plato, Moses and Ashoka, or Alexander and Caesar. Some trade goods, including silks, had made the passage across Central Asia, but as far as the Chinese knew, they were living in an oasis of civilization in a world of barbarians. Although there were eventually limited contacts with India, and Chinese technology was sometimes taken west by merchants and traders—especially during the Mongol era in the thirteenth century—the direct impact of the Han Empire and its successors on regions beyond East Asia was minimal until the development of global trading networks in the early modern era. Even then, old habits of thought continued in the minds of Chinese rulers long after they ceased to make sense. As late as 1792 the emperor Qianlong, in response to a delegation from Britain seeking to increase trade with China, wrote the following to King George III (who was undoubtedly still smarting after his loss of the American colonies): "Our Celestial empire possesses all things in prolific abundance and lacks no product within its own borders. There is therefore no need to import the manufactures of outside barbarians [that is, the British] in exchange for our own produce." The emperor did agree, however, to continue to allow silk, tea, and porcelain to be exported as a favor, bearing in mind "the lonely remoteness of your island, cut off from the world by the wastes of the sea."[3] Qianlong was quite wrong in his assessment of European power in the late eighteenth century, but for two thousand years, imperial China had enjoyed a remarkably stable, productive, and self-sufficient mode of existence.

We might still ask, however, how the Han Empire compared with other ancient regimes such as the Achaemenid Empire in Persia (c. 550–330 B.C.E.), the Mauryan Empire in India (321–183 B.C.E.), and the Roman Empire in the Mediterranean (27 B.C.E.–476 C.E.). Obviously each empire rested on the foundation of a massive, disciplined army capable of conquest, but even though there was little possibility of the Chinese copying from abroad—or vice versa—there were nevertheless a number of striking similarities. At the level of the central government, rulers gave themselves new titles that better reflected their new status; to be a mere king was not enough. In China there was now an emperor (*huangdi*), in Persia a "king of kings" (*shahanshah*); Mauryan sovereigns referred to themselves as "beloved of the gods," and Caesar Augustus of Rome (63 B.C.E.–14 C.E.) had himself proclaimed Augustus—"the revered one"—by the Senate. The authority of emperors was reinforced with propaganda. Like the First Emperor of China, both Darius of Persia (550–486 B.C.E.) and Ashoka in India (r. 269–232 B.C.E.) ordered the creation of rock inscriptions that praised their power and might. Augustus proved himself a master of political propaganda through his commissioning of statues, buildings, literature, and coins bearing his image.

In each empire, rulers adopted ideologies that supported their right to rule—in Han China it was Confucianism; in Persia, Zoroastrianism; in India, Buddhism; and in Rome, the civic Roman cults and eventually

Christianity. A class of professional administrators was created, and systems of regular reports, revenue collection, intelligence gathering, and bureaucratic oversight were all put in place. Ministers were appointed to oversee specific governmental functions. Each empire was divided into smaller administrative units headed by officials dispatched from the capital. Thus, the commanderies of China were matched by the twenty or so satrapies that made up the Persian Empire, along with the provinces of Mauryan India and Rome. To promote trade and communication, rulers established elaborate networks of roads; standardized weights, measures, and coinage; and encouraged the use of standard languages— the reformed Qin script in China and Aramaic in Persia. One might compare estimates of roads in Han China (20,000 miles), the Roman Empire (49,000 miles) and the United States interstate highway system today (46,700 miles)—though we should keep in mind the fact that China also had an extensive system of canals and waterways for transportation. The development of law codes, especially in Rome and China, promoted the ideals of universal justice and administrative efficiency.

Many of these parallels were the result of attempting to meet similar challenges in governing large, multiethnic territories. As Liu Bang discovered, regardless of one's intentions, it is impossible to run an empire on a three-sentence law code. But as is often the case in history, the differences among these empires may ultimately be more significant. China stands out as being more isolated than the other civilizations, and the Chinese knew of no rival literate cultures from which they could learn or to whom they might compare themselves. Slavery in China was not as widespread or as economically significant as elsewhere, and there was no caste system. Power in China was more centralized, with emperors challenged by fewer competing centers of authority. For instance, Emperor Wu never had to deal with a Senate or a Praetorian Guard as the Roman emperor did, and the notion of citizenship—with the common people voting and exercising legal rights—was never a part of Han political thought. Succession—the orderly transfer of power from one ruler to the next—was a perilous process in all four empires, but Chinese emperors were probably more secure in their position due to Chinese notions of sovereignty and filial piety. The Chinese military was more thoroughly under the control of the central government, and the Chinese state religion (consisting mostly of imperial sacrifices and offerings) was less significant than in other civilizations.

But perhaps the most important distinction between empires in China and elsewhere was that the Chinese bureaucracy was substantially larger and more developed. The *Han shu* reports that the number of officials serving in the central government down to the commandery level totaled 120,285. By contrast Rome, with a total population of about the same size, employed only about 30,000 civil servants throughout the empire. The Chinese scholar class had power and influence—much to the frustration of several emperors—but these officials were dedicated to the preservation of the central government; indeed, their identity had little meaning apart from it. An environment in which most potential critics of the government are deeply committed to traditional values lends itself to intense conservatism, and this was even more pronounced in a society that viewed respect for parents and ancestors as a primary virtue. In later dynasties, the ideal of the heroic scholar-bureaucrat became even more prominent, and education in the Confucian Classics came to be seen as the primary avenue to fame and fortune for young men. The twin ideals of public service and a Confucian-dominated intellectual life expressed through a single written language were crucial to the foundation of imperial China. It was a combination unique to China, and both elements were created in the Han Empire.

RECONSIDERING THE QIN AND THE HAN

Such was the glory of these classical states that later empires tried to borrow some of their luster. The Tang dynasty was modeled on the Han, just as the Parthians and Sasanid empires claimed the mantle of Persia, the Gupta portrayed itself as the restorer of the Mauryan regime, and Byzantium saw itself as a successor to Rome. Yet in the case of China, one puzzle remains. Since so much of the work of unification and centralization was done by the Qin dynasty, why was it not given credit? We have seen how Han rulers to a large extent adapted and continued Qin practices, but only the Han was celebrated in later eras. The Qin have been ridiculed and reviled for two thousand years.

In many ways, later dynasties were merely echoing the rationale offered by Han commentators themselves as they sought to explain why the Liu family was entitled to the Mandate of Heaven. In this book, we have for the most part adopted traditional Chinese ways of thinking about the difference between the Qin and Han empires: the First Emperor was cruel and oppressive, and in imposing change too harshly, he stirred up the resentment that quickly brought an end to his empire. By contrast, Han emperors were kind and benevolent (thereby gaining the Mandate), and thus were able to create a dynasty that lasted for four hundred years and eventually became the foundation for imperial China. This is a neat story, clear and simple, and later generations of Confucian scholars enjoyed telling of the dark days when the First Emperor burned books and persecuted Confucian scholars, even killing 460 of them. The tale allowed them to claim victim status, but also made their current position in Chinese society look like the victory of good over evil; Confucian morality was vindicated! Some modern scholars also suggest that the upstart first emperor of the Han dynasty, who began life as a commoner, needed to villainize the well-established aristocratic lineage of Qin in order to justify and legitimate his rule.

But the details of history are almost always more complicated than the prevailing conventional wisdom. Major historical events—like the establishment of the Han Empire—cannot be summed up with a single explanation. So far we have looked at this event by examining the basic timeline, the personalities of the major contenders, institutional innovations, technological advances, and changes in social relations. But Chinese notions of right and wrong—and how they apply to the Qin and the Han—have always been in the background. This perspective stems in part from our dependence on just a few Chinese sources—Sima Qian's *Shiji* in particular. In the last half century, however, even these ideas have come under increased scrutiny.

At the beginning of the twentieth century—a time when China was seen by Europeans and Americans as a backwards, impoverished nation— many Chinese blamed Confucianism for the sorry state of their country. Furthermore, after China narrowly escaped being carved up by Western imperialists in the late nineteenth century, by warlords in the 1920s and 1930s, by the Japanese invasion of World War II, and by the civil war that followed between the Communists and the Nationalists, tremendous value was placed on keeping China unified. Mao Zedong claimed credit for this feat, and in so doing, he was willing to reevaluate the achievement of the Qin. Sure, the First Emperor had been rough, but his brutality had been necessary, or even admirable, in the cause of a united China. Indeed, Mao himself was willing to go much further. In 1958, in a bout of boastful exaggeration, Mao declared:

> What does Qin Shihuang [the First Emperor] amount to? He buried
> only four hundred and sixty scholars alive; we have buried forty-six
> thousand scholars alive. Haven't we killed counterrevolutionary in-
> tellectuals? In my debates with some members of the minor demo-
> cratic parties, I told them: "You reviled us for being Qin Shihuangs.
> You're wrong. We have surpassed Qin Shihuang a hundredfold."[4]

The audience responded with laughter, but the words are nonetheless
chilling.

This tradition-overturning celebration of the Qin reached its climax
in the Anti-Lin Biao, Anti-Confucius campaign of the early 1970s
(which coincided with the discovery of the terra-cotta army next to the
First Emperor's tomb). The fervor of that political movement has sub-
sided, but there is still a willingness among many to put the Qin dynasty
in a more favorable light. The terra-cotta soldiers have become very famous, and many Chinese are proud of this cultural treasure, going so far
as to call it the "Eighth Wonder of the World." The 1996 film *The Emperor's Shadow* portrayed the First Emperor as a tragic figure who felt compelled to create an empire in order to bring hundreds of years of warfare
to an end. In these cases, the harshness of Qin rule is not doubted, but
it is seen as not necessarily a bad thing.

It is perhaps ironic that much of this discussion has been driven by
contemporary politics rather than historiography. The First Emperor's
burning of the books was motivated by his displeasure at scholars who
"spoke of the past in order to criticize the present."[5] In imperial China—
as well as in modern China, where power is as tightly held by the Com-
munist Party as it ever was by an emperor—speaking out in dissent was
dangerous. Intellectuals therefore often resorted to a kind of code in
which historical incidents and figures stood in for contemporary politics.
The Cultural Revolution (1966–1976)—an exceedingly brutal and de-
structive chapter in modern Chinese history—began when Mao decided
that a stage play about an upright Ming dynasty official who was dismissed from office was actually a veiled attack on his own firing of defense minister Peng Dehuai. So also the Anti-Lin Biao, Anti-Confucius
campaign seems to have been targeted at Premier Zhou Enlai (since Lin
Biao, like Confucius, was already dead by the time the movement began).
The party, of course, knows that stories of the past can be used in this
way, and has tried to commandeer historical discourse for its own ends.

And so it continues in a society where freedom of expression is still in question.

More recent criticisms of the traditional understanding of the Qin Empire, however, have been more firmly based on historical evidence. Many historians now suggest that the First Emperor may not have been as dictatorial as we had been led to believe by Han dynasty writers such as Lu Jia, Jia Yi, and Sima Qian (see Document 9). A careful reading of the *Shiji* indicates that the 460 unfortunate scholars were probably assorted magicians and specialists, not just Confucians (see Document 4), and they were simply executed rather than buried alive. Indeed, some modern historians suspect that Sima Qian's account may have been fabricated. The books that were proscribed and burned were only those held by private individuals; copies were kept safe in the imperial library for the use of court advisers. Thus, the greatest destruction to pre-imperial literature probably came not from the First Emperor's burning of the books but from Xiang Yu's sacking of the Qin capital. Archaeological discoveries of Qin laws reveal a legal system that was less harsh and irrational than previously thought (see Document 3). And it seems significant that rather than vigorously condemning the First Emperor, Liu Bang appointed twenty families to tend his grave in perpetuity. Only later in the dynasty was the First Emperor completely vilified.

Martin Kern has written an important study on the First Emperor's inscriptions, in which he points out that the language seems to draw on the entirety of early Chinese thought, not just Legalism (see Document 2). There also appears to have been quite a bit of continuity between the rituals used in the late Zhou, the Qin, and the Han. Furthermore, it is worth noting that a Confucian scholar like Shusun Tong could find employment both with the First Emperor and with Liu Bang. In a surprising reversal, Kern even suggests that the burning of the books may have been aimed at the rivals of the scholars of traditional learning, and that what we now consider Confucian orthodoxy may actually have benefited from the imposition of an official, accepted scholarship centered at the Qin court. As Kern notes, "Western Han historical writing on the Qin looks too suspicious in perfectly matching the new dynasty's need for political legitimation. . . . According to the growing archaeological evidence, even the very late pre-imperial Qin state, despite its administrative and legal reforms since the mid-fourth century, was a highly traditional political entity, certainly much more traditional—and much less violent—than the transmitted Han sources would have us believe."[6] The founder of the Han, on the other hand, was a commoner whose only justification for ruling was that he had the biggest army. It is not surprising that his associates soon crafted a version of history in which the Qin lost their right to rule through their immoral behavior.

In any event, we are still trying to understand what happened at the end of the third century B.C.E. when China became unified. The establishment of the Han Empire was obviously crucial for Chinese history, but it is important for the rest of the world as well. The People's Republic of China, the inheritor of that early empire, is today one of the most populous, powerful nations in the world. The story told in these pages is in many ways foreign to modern readers—we no longer live in a world dominated by crossbows and absolute monarchs—but there are nevertheless many details that will be familiar. Ambition, ideology, technological innovations, and organizational skills continue to move the world forward. In reading Chinese history, we can observe both long-term institutional and social processes as well as the interactions of vividly drawn, strong-willed individuals. If the actions of people long ago and far away sometimes seem strange and irrelevant, consider the following anecdote from 198 B.C.E.:

> The Weiyang Palace was completed. Gaozu [Liu Bang] held a great court gathering for the feudal lords and the assembled ministers, setting out wine in the front hall of the Weiyang Palace. Gaozu lifted his jade [drinking cup] and stood up to offer his father . . . a toast saying: "In the beginning you, sir, often considered me to have no prospects, unable to manage property, and not equal to Liu Zhong [Liu Bang's older brother] in ability. Now seeing those tasks which I have accomplished, whose have been more numerous, Zhong's or mine?" The assembled ministers in the hall all shouted "Long life!" and roared in their pleasure.[7]

A man who has conquered the world but still cannot quite get over the bruises of his childhood—the feeling that his father always liked his brother more—there is a scene for the ages.

NOTES

1. Watson's translation, in Burton Watson, trans., *Records of the Grand Historian, Han Dynasty*, 2 vols., rev. ed. (New York and Hong Kong: Renditions-Columbia University Press, 1993), 1:226–227.

2. Dubs, 1:259.

3. J.O.P. Brand, *Annals and Memoirs of the Court of Peking* (Boston: Houghton Mifflin, 1914), p. 326.

4. Li Yu-Ning, ed., *The First Emperor of China: The Politics of Historiography* (White Plains, NY: International Arts and Sciences Press, 1975), p. 1.

5. *Shiji*, 6.255; see Burton Watson, trans., *Records of the Grand Historian, Qin Dynasty* (New York and Hong Kong: Renditions-Columbia University Press, 1993), p. 54.

6. Martin Kern, *The Stele Inscriptions of Ch'in Shih-huang: Text and Ritual in Early Chinese Imperial Representation* (New Haven: America Oriental Society, 2000), pp. 155–156. Romanization changed to Pinyin.

7. Nienhauser's translation, in William H. Nienhauser, Jr., et al., *The Grand Scribe's Records* (Bloomington: Indiana University Press, 2002), 2:55. Slightly modified.

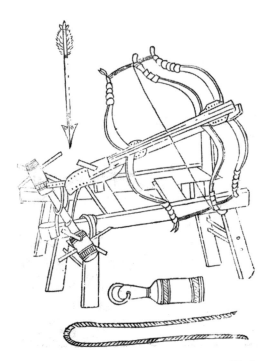

Figure 1. Crossbow. *Ming dynasty woodblock print from Wang Qi*, Sancai tuhui, *juan 6, p. 19.*

秦始皇帝

Figure 2. The First Emperor (Qin Shihuangdi, also known as King Zheng of Qin). *Ming dynasty woodblock print from Wang Qi*, Sancai tuhui, *juan 1, p. 46.*

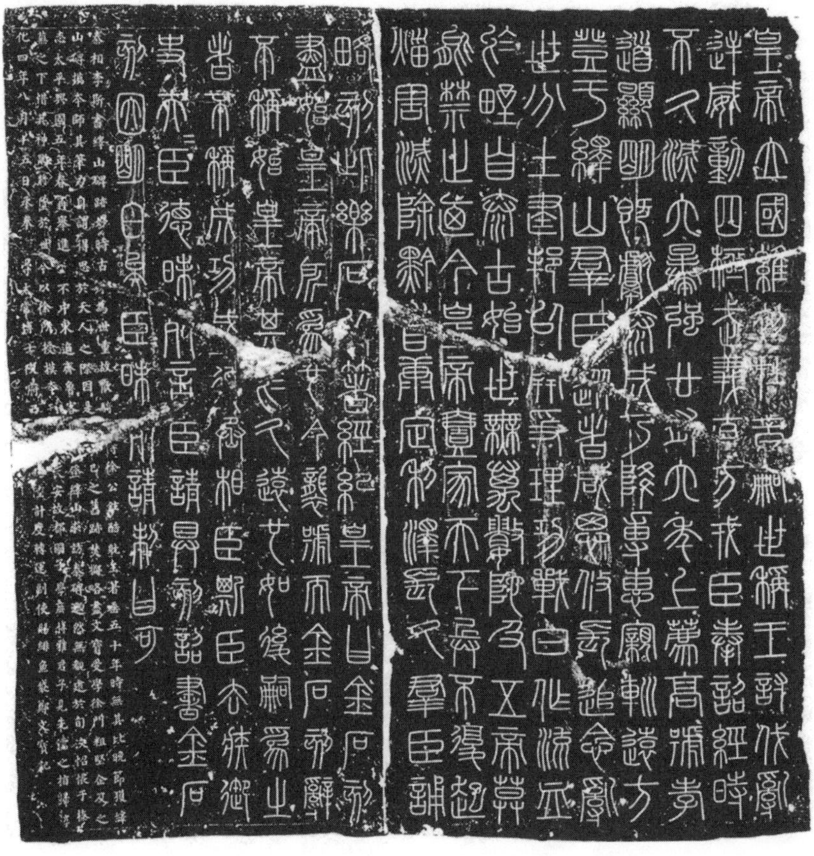

Figure 3. The 219 B.C.E. Mt. Yi inscription of the First Emperor of Qin (re-carved in 993 C.E.). *After Ledderose, Lothar, and Adele Schlombs, eds.,* Jenseits der Grosse Mauer: Der Erste Kaiser von China und seine Terrakotta-Armee *(Gütersloh: Bertelsmann Lexikon Verlag, 1990), plate 191. Daniel Schwartz, Lookat Photos, Zürich.*

Figure 4. Inscribed bronze standardized weight from the Qin dynasty. Anon., Historical Relics Unearthed in New China *(Beijing: Foreign Languages Press, 1972), fig. 79.*

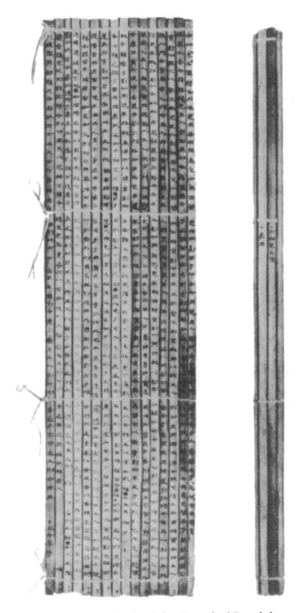

Figure 5. Bamboo book of the *Record of Ritual* discovered in 1959 in Wuwei, Gansu province. *Chen
Mengjia, et al.,* Wuwei Hanjian *(Beijing: Wenwu,
1964).*

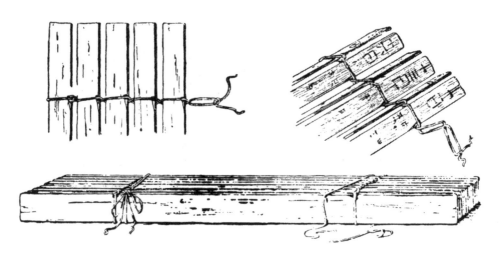

Figure 6. Method of binding wooden tablets. *Sir Aurel Stein, "Notes on Chinese Documents," New China Review 3 (1921): 243.*

圖　王　項

Figure 7. Xiang Yu, contender for the empire after the fall of Qin. *Ming dynasty woodblock print from Wang Qi,* Sancai tuhui, *juan 1, p. 48.*

漢 高 祖 像

Figure 8. Liu Bang (also known as Gaozu),
founder of the Han dynasty. *Ming dynasty*
woodblock print from Wang Qi, Sancai
tuhui, *juan 2, p. 4.*

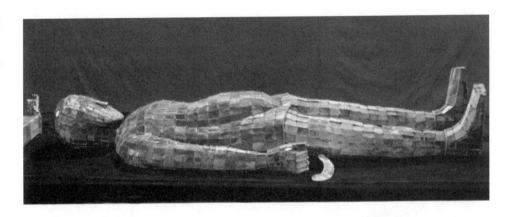

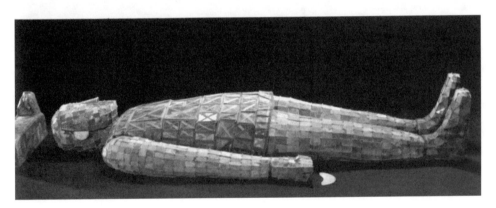

Figure 9. Han dynasty jade burial suits of Prince Liu Sheng and his wife. *Hebeisheng Wenwu guanlichu*, Mancheng Hanmu fajue baogao *(Beijing: Wenwu, 1980), vol. 2, plate 13.*

Figure 10. Farming and hunting scene from the Han dynasty. *Anon.*, Historical Relics Unearthed in New China *(Beijing: Foreign Languages Press, 1972), fig. 111.*

Figure 11. Han dynasty bronze shovel and hoe. *Anon.*, Historical Relics Unearthed in New China *(Beijing: Foreign Languages Press, 1972), fig. 83.*

耤田圖

Figure 12. Emperor's ceremonial plowing. *Qing dynasty woodblock print from Wang Zhen,* Nong shu, *juan 11, p. 2a.*

Figure 13. Reconstruction of Zhang Heng's seismograph. *Wang Zhenduo, "Han Zhang Heng Houfeng didong yi zaofa zhi tuize,"* Yanjing xuebao *20 (1936): 587.*

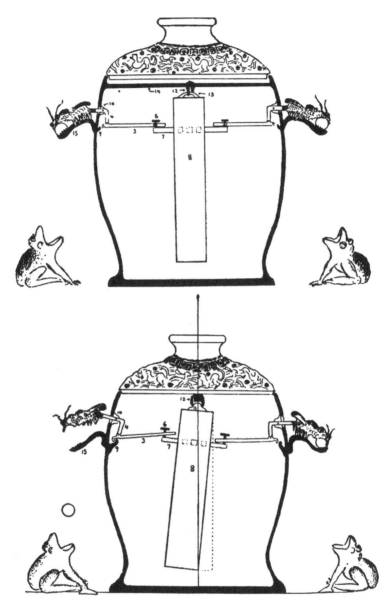

Figure 14. Seismograph reconstruction. *Wang Zhenduo, "Han Zhang Heng Houfeng didong yi zaofa zhi tuize,"* Yanjing xuebao 20 (1936): 589.

Figure 15. Han tomb figurine in chariot, most likely an aristocrat or an official. *Anon.*, Historical Relics Unearthed in New China *(Beijing: Foreign Languages Press, 1972)*, *fig. 93.*

Figure 16. Han tomb figurine of a woman. *Private collection*.

BIOGRAPHIES: THE PERSONALITIES OF THE QIN AND HAN EMPIRES

The names below are arranged by Pinyin Romanization. Wade-Giles transliterations appear in parentheses, followed by italicized informal pronunciation suggestions. When the subject has a biography in the *Shiji*, the chapter number is provided. Remember, the family name comes first in China, so that Han Xin, for example, might sometimes be referred to as "Han."

Chao Cuo (Ch'ao Ts'o; *Chow Tsoh*; d. 154 B.C.E.)— *Official*

Chao studied Legalist philosophy as a young man and voiced strong advocacy for the *Book of Documents*—one of the Five Classics—at the court of Emperor Wen. He submitted numerous memorials to the throne, arguing for the reduction of size of the marquisates and kingdoms, suggesting revisions to the law code, and proposing reforms in the military and agriculture (see Document 10). Emperor Wen implemented only a few of these ideas, but the heir apparent was very impressed with Chao's abilities. When he came to the throne as Emperor Jing, he appointed Chao imperial counselor; in that position, Chao was able to push through several changes to the legal code, including thirty new statutes mostly aimed at curbing the power of the feudal lords. Not surprisingly, Chao made many enemies among the powerful and well-connected, and even his own father tried to persuade him to adopt a more accommodating stance. When he refused, his father committed suicide rather than await the inevitable disaster that he felt was coming to the family. Within ten days, seven kingdoms revolted, with the kings claiming that Chao Cuo's stern policies had left them no alternative. In an attempt to pacify them (and with the encouragement of Chao's enemies at court), Emperor Jing had Chao executed. Unfortunately, this gesture did not stop the revolt, which was only overcome with thousands of imperial troops. Later on, Emperor Jing expressed regret for his decision to execute Chao Cuo. It is an indication of the fluid nature of Chinese philosophy at the time that an expert in what would later be considered a specifically Confucian Classic could be so closely associated with Legalist-style policies. (*Shiji*, ch. 101)

Chen She (Ch'en She; *Chun Shuh*; d. 208 B.C.E.)— *Rebel*

The leader of the first major revolt against the Qin dynasty, Chen began life as a common peasant. In 209, during the reign of the Second Emperor, he was appointed the head of nine hundred convicts who were being forcibly resettled. He was responsible for getting them to their destination, but when heavy rains washed out roads and it became apparent that they would not arrive on time (a failure for which the penalty was death), Chen led his men in revolt. He was able to win them over by fabricating supernatural signs and claiming to restore their feudal state of Chu. They killed their commanding officers from the Qin army and gathered some twenty thousand men as they attacked major cities (see Document 5). After initial successes, Chen proclaimed himself a king, and several of his subordinates quickly followed suit by claiming royal titles for themselves. Chen tried to keep his followers in line with executions and penalties, but in the end, he was forced to acknowledge many of their claims. He was finally assassinated by his chariot driver, who murdered Chen in an attempt to seek favor with the Qin authorities. Although Chen was king for only six months, the revolt he started continued until the dynasty fell, and several of the generals whom Chen had acknowledged as kings retained their positions into the early Han dynasty. In an acknowledgement of Chen's role in the establishment of the Han, in 195 Emperor Liu Bang appointed thirty families to provide continual offerings at his tomb. (*Shiji*, ch. 48)

Confucius (Chinese name: Kongzi; 551–479 B.C.E.)— *Philosopher*

Although Confucius lived long before the Han Empire, his ideas were crucial to providing a stable ideology that supported and restrained imperial power. Confucius was a minor noble in the state of Lu. According to some accounts, he briefly held the position of prime minister there, but most scholars regard this detail as quite unlikely. Though he wanted to serve in government, and indeed traveled widely seeking such a position, he failed in his quest and instead became a teacher. He was convinced that current social problems could be resolved by a return to the traditional morality of the early Zhou dynasty. To this end, he taught the importance of education, ritual, moral government, personal ethics, and social hierarchy—five areas that the humane person needed to balance and harmonize. Although in some ways a conservative, he also redefined the traditional notion of "gentleman" (originally, someone of aristocratic birth) to include anyone who acted with integrity and proper respect. He emphasized the literary tradition of Chinese culture and was long given credit for editing the five Confucian Classics—the *Book of Documents*, the *Book of Songs*, the *Spring and Autumn Annals*, the *Record of Ritual*, and the *Classic of Changes*—though modern scholarship has disputed this view. In 136 Emperor Wu, following the advice of Dong Zhongshu, established "Erudite Scholars" for each of these classics, and the study of these texts became the basis for the Imperial Academy founded in 124 for the training of future administrators. Confucius' teachings, combined with theories of yin and yang and the Five Phases, eventually became the official state ideology in the Han Empire. Many of his words to his students are preserved in the *Analects* (see Document 1). (*Shiji*, ch. 47)

Dong Zhongshu (Tung Chung-shu; *Doong Joong-shoe*; c. 179–105 B.C.E.)—*Philosopher*

Dong was one of the architects of Han Confucianism. He served as an "Erudite Scholar" under Emperor Jing, with a specialization in the *Spring and Autumn Annals*—one of the Confucian Classics. Under Emperor Wu, he was appointed chancellor to the kingdom of Jiangdu. He later became a counselor of the palace and wrote a treatise correlating natural disasters and the Mandate of Heaven. When a fire destroyed a temple dedicated to the founder of the Han dynasty, this book nearly cost Dong his life, since Dong generally attributed such natural disasters to the misconduct of the emperor. He served as prime minister in yet another kingdom, but when his political position became dangerous, he pleaded illness and retired to the capital to resume a life of scholarship. His most important book was the *Luxuriant Gems of the Spring and Autumn Annals*, which brought together Confucian ideas of morality and government with theories of yin and yang and the Five Phases. He was also interested in how earthly bodies and institutions mirror the patterns of nature and the heavens. (*Shiji*, ch. 121)

Dou, Empress (Tou; *Doe*; d. 135 B.C.E.)—*Empress and Dowager Empress (emperor's mother)*

Through a combination of luck and determination, Empress Dou became one of the most powerful women in the early Han Empire. She first came to court as an attendant of Empress Lü; later she was selected to be one of five consorts bestowed on each king. The king to whom she was assigned eventually became Emperor Wen, and because the four sons of his deceased primary wife had all died young, his oldest male heir (the future Emperor Jing) was the son of Lady Dou, who then became Empress Dou. She requested posthumous titles for her parents and had a key role in rescuing her younger brother who had been kidnapped as a small boy. Her two brothers and a cousin all became marquises. Empress Dou read memorials to the throne during the reign of her son, and she was a major participant in discussions of personnel and policy. She was, however, partial to Daoism and made all her relatives, including her son, study the teachings of Laozi and the Yellow Emperor. The relatively quiet reigns of Emperors Wen and Jing are often ascribed to her influence. She outlived both emperors, dying in the sixth year of the reign of Emperor Wu. Only after her death was he able to begin his aggressive domestic and foreign policies. (*Shiji*, ch. 49)

First Emperor (Chinese title: Qin Shi Huangdi or Ch'in Shih Huang-ti [First August Emperor of the Qin], *Cheen Sure Hwang-dee*; previously known as King Zheng of Qin; 259–210 B.C.E.)—*Qin Emperor*

The First Emperor became king of the state of Qin in 246 at the age of thirteen. Qin already had a dominant position among the warring states, and over the next twenty-five years, the king—with the aid of his advisers and generals—plotted and fought to conquer all of China. When his goal was accomplished in 221, he proclaimed himself the "First Emperor" and then initiated dramatic reforms intended to centralize his authority and unify his territories. These reforms included standardizing weights, measures, coinage, laws, and the written language. He organized China into commanderies (similar to provinces), forcibly relocated thousands of people, and began massive building programs constructing roads, canals, walls, magnificent palaces, and his remarkable mausoleum. When scholars criticized his policies, basing their comments on precedents drawn from classical texts, he ordered the burning of the books and, according to traditional sources, executed 460 dissenting scholars. The First Emperor toured China five times and set up many inscriptions praising his own accomplishments (see Document 2). Although he patronized magicians who promised to reveal the secret to long life, he died suddenly after ruling the Qin Empire for only a decade. One of his advisors memorably described him as follows: "The king of Qin, with his arched nose and long eyes, puffed-out chest like a hawk and voice of a jackal, is a man of scant mercy who has the heart of a tiger or a wolf. When he is in difficulty he readily humbles himself before others, but when he has gotten his way, then he thinks nothing of eating others alive" (Watson's trans., *Records, Qin*, p. 38–39). (*Shiji*, ch. 6)

Han Xin (Han Hsin; *Hahn Sheen*; d. 197 B.C.E.)— *General and King*

Han Xin began life with few obvious talents. He failed at farming, government, and business, and eventually joined Xiang Yu's rebellion. Xiang Yu ignored his military advice, so he joined Liu Bang. When Liu also ignored him, he ran away again only to be brought back by Xiao He, one of Liu's advisors who had been very impressed with him. Xiao He urged

Liu to promote Han Xin to major general, and once in that position, his skill on the battlefield proved crucial to Liu Bang's success (see Document 7). Indeed, his loyalty during difficult times was probably what made the difference as to whether the next emperor would be Liu Bang or Xiang Yu. When Han proclaimed himself king of Qi in 203, Liu Bang was furious and would have attacked had not Zhang Liang reminded Liu of how much he still needed Han's support. Nevertheless, after the founding of the Han dynasty, Liu showed his appreciation by making Han Xin the king of Chu. There was still, however, considerable tension between the central government and the semi-independent kingdoms of the early Han, and when Liu Bang suspected that Han Xin might revolt, he had him arrested and brought to court. Later the emperor pardoned him and made him marquis of Huaiyin. Five years later, Han Xin did plot secretly with another rebelling noble. While Liu Bang was fighting in the field, Empress Lü tricked Han Xin into coming to court; when he arrived, she had him beheaded. Liu only learned of this after he had put down the rebellion and returned to the capital. Sima Qian reports that Liu Bang was both pleased and saddened by the news. (*Shiji*, ch. 92)

Li Si (Li Ssu; *Lee Suh;* c. 280–208 B.C.E.)—*Qin Official*

A native of the state of Chu, Li Si studied under the Confucian philosopher Xunzi. He thought that Qin was the most powerful of the major states at the time, and being ambitious himself, he offered his services to the king of Qin. Li became the commandant of justice and worked closely with the king for twenty years, as he centralized his state and expanded his territory. Finally, in 221, Qin defeated the last of its rivals and the king proclaimed himself the First Emperor, with Li Si as his chancellor. Li Si's main concern was power, and he is usually thought of today as a Legalist. Certainly his advice included strong condemnations of feudalism, and he called for the termination of local standards of weights, measures, coinage, laws, and scripts in favor of a unified standard followed by the whole empire. On two occasions, he forcefully argued against proposals to establish a new aristocracy, and he was the author of a plan to unify thought by outlawing the general circulation of all books of history and philosophy, including the Confucian Classics (see Document 4). When the First Emperor died suddenly in 210, Li Si plotted with Zhao

Gao to hide the emperor's death and change the heir apparent. Their strategy succeeded, but when the Second Emperor proved incompetent, Li Si tried to reason with him. Zhao Gao arranged for Li Si to speak with him at the worst possible times, and when the emperor became exasperated, Zhao persuaded him that Li was disloyal. Li Si was arrested and beaten by Zhao Gao's men until he confessed to various fictitious crimes. Zhao then falsified reports to support the allegations, and the Second Emperor ordered that Li Si be cut in two at the waist. (*Shiji*, ch. 87)

Liu Bang (Liu Pang; *Leo Bahng*; also known as Liu Ji [Liu Chi; *Leo Gee*], Gaozu [Kao-tsu; *Gao-zoo*; "Exalted Ancestor"], and the King of Han; d. 195 B.C.E.)—*Han Emperor*

The founder of the Han Empire was one of only two emperors in Chinese history who began life as a peasant (the other was the founder of the Ming dynasty in the fourteenth century). In the chaos at the end of the Qin Empire, Liu Bang went from village head to bandit to rebel, joining forces with two other rebels, Xiang Liang and his nephew Xiang Yu. In time, Xiang Yu and Liu Bang became the two most important rebel generals. Liu was the first to conquer the heartland of Qin though Xiang Yu managed to gain the upper hand politically. Xiang took the lead of the now victorious rebel forces and divided the empire in 206. He assigned Liu to be the king of Han, but when Xiang Yu marched his armies west back to his native region of Chu, Liu grabbed the strategically important territory of Qin. There followed four years of civil war in which Liu finally defeated Xiang Yu and proclaimed himself emperor of a new dynasty, the Han. Liu Bang continued many of the administrative and legal innovations of the Qin, but he was forced to grant large territories as kingdoms to some of his followers. He lived for another seven years, during which he continued to lead his armies in battle—sometimes against the Xiongnu nomads in the north and sometimes against kings in revolt. The empire was still unified at his death, but it was far from stable. The Later Han historian Ban Gu described Liu's character as follows: "In his early life, Gaozu did not cultivate literary studies, but by nature he was intelligent and penetrating. He liked to make plans and was able to listen to others. From a superintendent of a gate or a man exiled to the frontier upwards, anyone who came to see him was treated as an old friend" (Dubs' trans., in *History of the Former Han Dynasty*, 1:146). (*Shiji*, ch. 8)

Lü, Empress (Lü; Lyoo; d. 180 B.C.E.)—*Empress and Dowager Empress*

Empress Lü was the only woman to rule like an emperor during the Han dynasty. During the time that her young son, Emperor Hui, was on the throne and during the brief reigns of two more child emperors—a period of fifteen years—she was in firm control of China. The Han histories tell us that her father had the ability to foresee the future by studying a person's face. He recognized Liu Bang's promise while he was still a commoner and, over his wife's objections, arranged a marriage between Liu and his own daughter. This young woman would become Empress Lü when Liu became emperor, and she bore him a son and a daughter. The empress aided her husband in his quest for empire and punished ministers and generals whom she suspected of disloyalty. She also worked hard to promote the interests of her family. Though her son held the position of heir apparent, Liu Bang had flirted with the idea of replacing him with the son of a concubine, Lady Qi (*Chee*). Empress Lü strenuously resisted and then, after Liu's death, poisoned the boy and tortured his mother. She enjoyed considerable power when her son became the next emperor and then, after his death, when she arranged for two of her infant grandchildren to become the next two emperors. Apparently there was some doubt as to whether these boys were actually related to her, but in any case she ruled China as regent while they were alive. Perhaps because she was nervous about the legitimacy of their claims, she moved to place members of her own clan in key military and administrative positions. Indeed, it looked for a while as if the Lü clan would replace the Liu clan as the imperial family. But after her death, several ministers planned a coup that massacred her kinsmen and placed Emperor Jing (another of Liu Bang's sons) on the throne. Though noted for her ruthlessness and cruelty toward those who threatened her status, her reign is remembered as a time of peace and rest after the upheavals and violence surrounding the establishment of the Han dynasty. She lowered taxes and removed from the law code some of the more severe corporal punishments. (*Shiji*, ch. 9)

Second Emperor (Chinese name: Huhai; *Who hi*; d. 207 B.C.E.)—*Qin Emperor*

Although Huhai was a younger son of the First Emperor of Qin, through the plotting of Li Si and Zhao Gao he displaced the heir apparent and became the Second Emperor at the age of twenty-one. In that position he proved utterly incompetent. He was cruel—for example, he executed all the craftsmen who had worked on his father's tomb to prevent them from disclosing its secret treasures—and extravagant. Under the influence of Zhao Gao, he terrorized members of the imperial family, officials, and generals alike. All this left him with little support at the time of Chen She's revolt. As the rebellion grew, Zhao Gao advised the Second Emperor to stay hidden and allow Zhao to relay his instructions to the officials. In this way, Zhao Gao gradually gained control of the government, to the extent that when he presented a deer to the emperor and claimed that it was a horse, most of the courtier agreed with him rather than with the Second Emperor, who scoffed at the obvious mistake. As the empire started to collapse, Zhao began to worry about his position, and he organized a palace coup that took the life of the Second Emperor. He had ruled China for three years. (No *Shiji* biography, but details of the Second Emperor's life can be found in the "Basic Annals of the First Emperor of Qin," *Shiji*, ch. 6.)

Shang Yang (*Shahng Yahng*; sometimes known as Lord Shang; d. 338 B.C.E.)—*Early Qin Official*

Though he lived a century before the First Emperor, Shang Yang's Legalist reforms in the state of Qin were crucial to placing that kingdom on the path that led eventually to the Qin Empire. Shang was originally from the state of Wei, but he immigrated to Qin in search of a ruler who would put his ideas into practice. When he won the trust of Duke Xiao (r. 361–338) of Qin, he was able to implement his policies, including organizing the families of the state into mutually responsible groups of five and ten households, doubling the taxes on families with adult sons still living at home, offering tax incentives for successful farmers, decreasing the influence of aristocrats, and establishing a new system of government rank based on military merit, not birth. All people were treated equally under the laws, those who aided criminals were executed, and harsh penalties were freely used (when the heir apparent broke the law, however, his tutor was punished in his stead and his nose was cut off). The country was divided into thirty-one counties, and weights and measures were made uniform. Similar policies had been experimented with elsewhere in China, but Shang was the first to implement them consistently and on a broad scale. He also allowed no criticism or discussion of his new laws. After ten years, Qin was wealthy, militarily powerful, and free of internal disputes. It was not surprising that the First Emperor based his reorganization of all of China on Shang Yang's model. Unfortunately, this consolidation of state power and the intimidation of the populace left many people resentful. When Duke Xiao died and the heir apparent became the new ruler, Shang Yang was accused by friends of the heir's tutor of plotting revolt. When he fled, he discovered that his own laws against helping fugitives were used against him. Other states either feared or hated Qin, and so would not take him in. In the end he was killed, and his body torn in two by chariots to serve as a warning for others. In accordance with his policy of mutual responsibility, his entire family was executed as well. (*Shiji*, ch. 68)

Shusun Tong (*Shoe-swun Toeng*; d. c. 190 B.C.E.)— *Confucian Scholar/Adviser in Both Qin and Han*

Shusun Tong was from Confucius' native state of Lu and was an expert in traditional Chinese literary and ritual texts. This expertise would qualify him as a Confucian, but this was before the orthodoxy of Han Confucianism had been established. Shusun was remarkably proficient at adapting to the times, which is why he was able to serve the First Emperor, the Second Emperor, Xiang Liang, the Righteous Emperor of Chu, and Liu Bang all in turn. He served as an erudite at the Qin capital, but when the Second Emperor was upset at the initial reports of a massive rebellion, Shusun deceitfully assured him that it was only a case of local banditry and then fled the court as fast as he could. Because he knew that Liu Bang hated Confucians, he put away his scholarly robes and recommended outlaws and ruffians for service, over the objections of his students. He explained to them that in the midst of a civil war, literary arts were not the highest priority, but then after the empire was at peace, he was able to get many of his followers appointed to office. He created court rituals for the Han (despite the complaints of many scholars who worried that he was putting practicality over historical accuracy), and in so doing he was immensely important in establishing the Han conception of imperial sovereignty. He is also a key figure in the general continuity of Qin and Han practices. (*Shiji*, ch. 99)

Sima Qian (Ssu-ma Ch'ien; *Sue-ma Chyen;* c. 145–86 B.C.E.)—*Historian*

Sima Qian was the first historian of China. Although there had been earlier chronicles and collections of stories about the past, Sima was the first person to write a history of China under his own name, and the account that he produced—the *Shiji* (Records of the Grand Historian)—provided a model for historians over the next two thousand years. Sima Qian's father, Sima Tan (d. 110)—who was a court astrologer to Emperor Wu—had started a history, and on his deathbed he begged his son to continue his efforts. It is not clear how much Sima Tan had actually written, but when Sima Qian inherited the office of court astrologer, he continued writing a comprehensive history of China, from its legendary beginnings to his own age. Unfortunately, Sima Qian became entangled in court politics when he spoke up for a general who had been captured in fighting the Xiongnu. Emperor Wu was furious and sentenced Sima to castration, a standard punishment for crimes of a serious nature. Although it would have been considered more honorable for Sima Qian to have committed suicide (since eunuchs could not be considered filial sons), Sima accepted his humiliating punishment so that he could have time to finish his history. His work has been read, admired, and imitated ever since. The *Shiji* is a significant cultural expression of the trend of Sima Qian's time toward political and intellectual consolidation. Just as Han emperors had worked to bring "all under heaven" under their control, so Sima tried to bring together all of China's history, geography, and culture within a single work. Sima himself believed that having met failure and disgrace in his own life, he was writing primarily for future generations. In this ambition, he certainly succeeded. (*Shiji*, ch. 130 [Sima Qian's autobiography])

Wei Zifu (Wei Tzu-fu; *Way Dzuh-foo*; d. 91 B.C.E.)— *Empress*

Wei Zifu is notable as a woman who rose from the rank of slave to that of empress, and whose elevation allowed for the ascent of her male kin to some of the highest positions in the land. She started from very humble beginnings as a singing girl in the household of Emperor Wu's elder sister. When Wu's primary wife failed to produce a son, his sister invited him to her house and introduced him to ten women of good families. Finding all of them uninteresting, he was instead attracted to her servant Wei Zifu. His sister sent Wei to the palace, where she enjoyed the emperor's attentions and escaped several attempts on her life by jealous rivals. In 130, Emperor Wu's primary wife was accused of practicing witchcraft and deposed (about three hundred people were implicated and executed). Wei Zifu gave birth to Emperor Wu's first son two years later. She was immediately named as the new empress, and her son became heir apparent in 122. This should have secured her position, but there was bitter rivalry between the families of Wei Zifu and Li Furen, a minor consort of Emperor Wu's who had also borne a son. Li Furen had died young, and the emperor was heartbroken. He hired sorcerers to try to communicate with her spirit, and he favored her family members. In particular, her oldest brother became a powerful general. At the same time, Wei's younger brother and a nephew were made senior generals. The Wei clan was associated with the aggressive foreign policies that had turned out to be ruinously expensive, and in 91 the Li family tried to supplant the Wei family in influence. Sources suggest that the Li family planted evidence in the rooms of the heir apparent that would create the appearance of the heir's disloyalty to his father, Emperor Wu. An official connected to the Li family tried to arrest the heir apparent while the emperor was away at the summer palace. The heir apparent then launched his own attack against the imperial guards, and the fighting spread to the streets of the capital. Some ten thousand people died in the conflict, the Wei family was defeated, Wei Zifu committed suicide, and her son, who had been heir apparent for over thirty years, was killed. In the aftermath, more Wei relatives and several senior officials were executed. Soon, however, sentiment turned against the Li family, and several of their members and supporters were also put to death. The situation became worse when Li Furen's brother (the general) surrendered to the Xiongnu.

Though both families were nearly wiped out, one of Li Furen's grandsons was later emperor for about a month, and Wei Zifu's great-grandson reigned as Emperor Xuan (74–49). (*Shiji*, ch. 49)

Wu, Emperor (Wu; Woo; 156–87 B.C.E., r. 141–87 B.C.E.)—*Han Emperor*

After the relatively quiet eras of Emperors Wen and Jing, Emperor Wu's remarkable fifty-four year reign was a period of aggressive domestic and foreign activity. Wu was fifteen when his father Emperor Jing died, and at the time he succeeded him as emperor, the court was dominated by his Daoist-inclined grandmother, Empress Dou. After her death six years later in 135, Emperor Wu began to curtail the power of the kings and marquises who had been granted semi-independent territories within the Han Empire. He also sought to expand the borders of the empire by sending armies northeast into Korea, north into Mongolia, west into Central Asia, southwest into Tibet and Burma, and south to Vietnam (using modern names for these regions). In order to pay for these massive campaigns, he instituted government monopolies on salt, iron, and alcohol; established a government system of grain distribution and trade; centralized the minting of coins; and allowed the sale of ranks and titles. He patronized the arts and literature, reformed imperial sacrifices, and made several imperial tours of China to survey his domains. All this would seem to make Emperor Wu a Legalist emperor on par with the First Emperor of Qin, but at the same time Wu heeded the advice of Dong Zhongshu and proclaimed Confucianism the official ideology of the state. He appointed erudite scholars who specialized in the Five Confucian Classics, and in 124 he established the Imperial Academy for the training of future bureaucrats in Confucian philosophy. The Han Empire probably reached the height of its power and prosperity about 105. Unfortunately, the later years of Emperor Wu's reign were marred by economic problems and deadly infighting at the court. (The *Shiji* chapter on Emperor Wu has been lost, though it is not clear how candidly Sima Qian could have written about his own emperor. In any case, the *Han shu* includes the "Annals of Emperor Wu," ch. 6.)

Xiang Yu (Hsiang Yü; *Shee-ong You;* 233–202 B.C.E.)—*Rebel General, Hegemon-King, and Rival to Liu Bang*

The Xiang clan, who had served for generations as generals in the state of Chu, was one of the families reduced to commoner status when the First Emperor did away with the aristocracy of the feudal states. Not surprisingly, when Chen She began his revolt in 209, Xiang Yu and his uncle Xiang Liang also launched an uprising by assassinating a Qin governor. Xiang Yu was twenty-four at the time. Xiang Liang quickly became a major leader in the rebellion, and after his death, Xiang Yu took over. As the one rebel general who could consistently defeat imperial troops, Xiang rose to a preeminent position. After he engineered the surrender of the Qin's commanding general, Xiang took possession of the capital, executed the last Qin ruler, and unified China once again. Rather than ruling as an emperor, however, he returned to the feudal pattern by appointing eighteen of the rebel generals as deputy kings. He himself took the title of hegemon-king, and he named a grandson of the last king of Chu the "Righteous Emperor"—a position with little power and even less security. Within a year, Xiang Yu had the man assassinated. He appointed Liu Bang to be the king of Han, even though according to an earlier agreement Liu should have gotten the "Land between the Passes," that is, the territory of the old Qin capital (Xianyang). Xiang Yu decided to reign from his home territory of Chu, but when he marched east with his troops, Liu seized possession of the Qin capital that had originally been promised to him, and other kings began grabbing territory as well. Xiang Yu turned his army around and began fighting again, but after four years, most of China had gone over to the side of Liu Bang. After his troops were surrounded and defeated, Xiang Yu committed suicide on the battlefield at the age of thirty-one. Though Xiang Yu was undoubtedly the better military strategist, in the end he lost the war—most likely because he was less adept than Liu Bang at taking advice and rewarding his followers (though later in the Han Empire, people claimed that Liu's victory also had something to do with the Mandate of Heaven). (*Shiji*, ch. 7)

Xiao He (Hsiao Ho; *Shau Huh*; d. 193 B.C.E.)— *Official*

Xiao He was one of Liu Bang's oldest and closest associates. When he was a local official in the Qin government and Liu was still a commoner, he treated Liu with particular graciousness. He supported Liu when he first rebelled, then served him faithfully thereafter as his chief civil administrator. While Liu Bang was away fighting, Xiao made sure that in his territories taxes were collected, laws were enforced, and supplies and recruits were gathered and sent to the battlefield. On several occasions when Liu had lost major conflicts, he was able to continue only because of reinforcements sent by Xiao He. In addition to being a capable administrator, Xiao was also remarkably astute. He had the foresight to seize the maps and population records of the Qin government while Liu Bang held the capital, which enabled him to assess the resources under his control and later allowed the Han regime to make a relatively smooth transition from the Qin administration. He was the principal adapter of the Qin laws and the first to recognize Han Xin's talent; in addition, he was able to retain Liu's trust even though Liu could be very suspicious of subordinates who seemed too talented or too popular. When Liu founded the Han dynasty, he gave the highest rewards and honor to Xiao He over the objections of some of his generals who protested that they had done the actual fighting. Liu knew, however, that without Xiao He's loyal support, he would not have been able to accomplish anything. (*Shiji*, ch. 53)

Zhang Liang (Chang Liang; *Johng Lee-ong*; d. 185 B.C.E.)—*Strategist*

Zhang Liang was a wandering swordsman who had once tried to assassinate the First Emperor. He eventually joined Liu Bang's rebellion and became his chief strategist. He devised several schemes that saved Liu's life and ensured the defeat of his enemies. Two examples will suffice. First, when Han Xin without authorization proclaimed himself "acting king" of Qi in 203, Liu Bang started raging at the envoy who had brought the news. Zhang Liang stepped on Liu's foot under the table and reminded him that he could not afford to lose Han's support. Liu quickly changed gears, explaining that he was upset because Han Xin deserved to be made an actual king, not just an "acting king." Second, shortly after Liu Bang became emperor in 202, there were many at court who were worried that they would not get all the rewards promised to them during the many years of civil war. Zhang asked Liu which of his followers he hated the most, then advised him to reward that man first. As expected, when the others saw that even Liu's enemies were being treated fairly, they stopped worrying. After the founding of the Han dynasty, Liu singled out Zhang Liang—along with Xiao He and Han Xin—as one of the key elements of his success in defeating Xiang Yu, despite the fact that ill health had generally kept Zhang away from the battlefield. Later, Zhang proved invaluable to Empress Lü when he came up with a plan to prevent Liu Bang from changing the heir apparent (Empress Lü's son). As Liu once said, "When it comes to sitting within the tents of command and devising strategies that will assure victory a thousand miles away, I am no match for Zhang Liang" (Watson's trans., *Records*, Han, 1:76). Zhang's discernment and cleverness were indeed uncanny, though he ascribed his success to a secret book of military strategy that a mysterious old man had given him. (*Shiji*, ch. 55)

Zhao Gao (Chao Kao; *Jau Gau*; d. 207 B.C.E.)—*Eunuch*

One of the most notorious characters in Chinese history, Zhao Gao was a eunuch at the court of the First Emperor. When the Emperor died unexpectedly in 210, Zhao plotted with the prime minister Li Si to hide the fact of his death and forge orders to replace the heir apparent with someone they could manipulate more easily. They were successful in engineering the death of the heir and placing the Second Emperor on the throne. Zhao Gao dominated the Second Emperor, encouraging him to act harshly and using him to destroy his own enemies and rivals—including Li Si. Zhao had convinced the Second Emperor to stop meeting with his officials, and then gradually took over the governing of the empire himself. In this way he moved from chief of the inner court to chancellor, and without the oversight of the emperor, there were no restraints on his actions. The imperial family and other officials were all terrified of Zhao's power, a situation that made it much more difficult to deal with the rebellions that were breaking out all over China. Zhao had kept the emperor uninformed about the revolts, but as rebel successes mounted, he was afraid he would be blamed for not stopping them. When Liu Bang's forces were advancing on the capital, Zhao staged a coup against the Second Emperor, forcing him to commit suicide. After the Second Emperor's death, Zhao tried to become emperor himself. When the court refused to support him, he set up a nephew of the Second Emperor as the king of Qin (dropping the now inappropriate title of emperor). This was the ruler who surrendered to Liu Bang about a month later, but only after stabbing and killing Zhao Gao first. (No *Shiji* biography, but details of Zhao Gao's life can be found in the "Basic Annals of the First Emperor of Qin," *Shiji*, ch. 6, and the "Biography of Li Si," *Shiji*, ch. 87.)

PRIMARY DOCUMENTS OF EARLY CHINA

DOCUMENT 1
Confucius on Government (c. 500 B.C.E.)

Confucius lived long before the Han Empire, but his teachings on ethics, ritual, and, especially, moral government were crucial to the success of the Han and to later imperial China. Young Chinese boys learned to read by memorizing his words, and for nearly two thousand years, aspiring students were tested in their knowedge of the Confucian Classics as part of the famed civil service exams. The comments below are from the Analects, a collection of Confucius' words put together by his students after his death. The sayings in the Analects are not organized by theme, so these passages on proper governing are drawn from various places in the text.

The Master said, "If the people be led by laws, and uniformity sought to be given them by punishments, they will try to avoid the punishment, but have no sense of shame. If they be led by virtue, and uniformity sought to be given them by the rules of propriety [li], they will have the sense of shame, and moreover will become good." (2.3)

Lord Ji Kang asked how to cause the people to reverence their ruler, to be faithful to him, and to go on to nerve themselves to virtue. The Master said, "Let him preside over them with gravity;—then they will reverence him. Let him be final and kind to all;—then they will be faithful to him. Let him advance the good and teach the incompetent;—then they will eagerly seek to be virtuous." (2.20)

Zigong [a student] asked about government. The Master said, "The requisites of government are that there be sufficiency of food, sufficiency of military equipment, and the confidence of the people in their ruler." Zigong said, "If it cannot be helped, and one of these must be dispensed with, which of the three should be foregone first?" "The military equipment," said the Master. Zigong again asked, "If it cannot be helped, and one of the remaining two must be dispensed with, which of them should be foregone?" The Master answered, "Part with the food. From of old, death has been the lot of all men; but if the people have no faith in their rulers, there is no standing for the state." (12.7)

Duke Jing, of Qi, asked Confucius about government. Confucius replied, "There is government, when the prince is prince, and the minister is minister; when the father is father, and the son is son." "Good!" said the duke; "if, indeed, the prince be not prince, the minister not minister, the father not father, and the son not son, although I have my revenue, can I enjoy it?" (12.11)

Lord Ji Kang, distressed about the number of thieves in the state, inquired of Confucius how to do away with them. Confucius said, "If you, sir, were not covetous, although you should reward them to do it, they would not steal." (12.18)

Lord Ji Kang asked Confucius about government, saying, "What do you say to killing the unprincipled for the good of the principled?" Confucius replied, "Sir, in carrying on your government, why should you use killing at all? Let your evinced desires be for what is good, and the people will be good. The relation between superiors and inferiors is like that between the wind and the grass. The grass must bend, when the wind blows across it." (12.19)

When the Master went to Wei, Ran Qiu acted as driver of his carriage. The Master observed, "How numerous are the people!" Ran Qiu said, "Since they are thus numerous, what more shall be done for them?" "Enrich them," was the reply. "And when they have been enriched, what more shall be done?" The Master said, "Teach them." (13.9)

Source: From the *Analects.* Translated by James Legge, *Confucian Analects, the Great Learning, and the Doctrine of the Mean* (Oxford: Clarendon Press, 1893).

DOCUMENT 2
The First Emperor's Inscription at Langya (219 B.C.E.)

After the king of Qin became the First Emperor in 221, he began a series of five grand tours around the empire. On each one he ordered the carving of propaganda inscriptions that glorified his reign. These are significant because they provide insight into what he himself thought of the unification of China. Not surprisingly, he claims to have brought peace and happiness to the world, with a harmony that extended even to the animals in his realm. His emphasis on laws and regulations is expected, but he also professes concern for the common people (the "black-haired ones"). The following inscription is from his second tour, when he reached the eastern limits of his empire on the coast of the Yellow Sea (see Figure 3 for another inscription of the First Emperor).

In his twenty-eighth year [219], the Emperor began to lay the foundations of the state.

He rectified the laws, by which all things are regulated, human affairs are clarified, and fathers and sons united.

Being sagacious, intelligent, benevolent, and righteous, he manifested the Way and reason.

Traveling to the east to tend the eastern lands, he paid visits to soldiers and warriors. Having finished these matters, he then came to the sea.

As the Emperor is industrious, he toils at the basic tasks.

Exalting agriculture and suppressing the non-essential [commerce], he enriches the black-haired ones.

The people under the vast heavens devote their minds to and unite in their goals.

With regard to implements, measurements have been unified; in writings, characters have been standardized.

Wherever the sun and the moon shine, wherever boat and cart can reach, People all live out their allotted span, and each is satisfied.

To initiate things in accord with the times is what this Emperor does.

To reform and regulate the divergent customs, he crosses waters and transverses lands.

He mourns for and relieves the black-haired, day and night unremittingly.

He eliminates the dubious and fixes the laws, thus the people all know what to observe.
The regional lords are assigned their allotted duties, governing of all sorts is routine and easy.
Whatever he does or undoes is absolutely appropriate, everything is done as distinctly as if it had been marked out.

As the Emperor is bright, he comes to inspect the four quarters.
Superiors and inferiors, the noble and the mean, none transgressed his own rank.
The evil and depraved are not tolerated, all strive to be upright and good.
In things great or small the utmost effort is put forth, no one ventures to be idle and negligent.
The people far or near, eminent or obscure,
Strive to be respectful and sedate, decent and upright,
Sincere and loyal, and to have their enterprises endure.

As the Emperor is virtuous, he consoles and pacifies the people at the four points of the compass.
Punishing the disorderly and eliminating the harmful, he promotes the interest of the state and brings about bliss.
He regulates manual labor according to the seasons, and all walks of life prosper.
The black-haired live in peace, with no use for weapons and armor.
The six-kins care for each other, and there are no outlaws or thieves at all.
Each merrily receives the imperial teachings, and thoroughly understands the forms and the norms.

Within the six paired directions [above and below, north and south, east and west] is the Emperor's land.
To the west it crosses Liusha, to the south it ends where houses face north.
To the east it encompasses the Eastern Sea, and to the north it stretches beyond Daxia.
As far as one can find traces of human beings, everyone has submitted.
His merits surpass those of the Five Emperors, and his kindness extends to cows and horses.
All things receive his favor, and live peacefully in their own abode.

Source: From the "Basic Annals of the First Emperor of Qin," *Shiji*, ch. 6. Translated by William H. Nienhauser, Jr., et al., *The Grand Scribe's Records* (Bloomington: Indiana University Press, 1994), 1:140–141. Reprinted with permission of the publisher.

DOCUMENT 3
Excerpts from Qin Laws (c. 215 B.C.E.)

In 1975 a tomb was discovered that contained several texts from the Qin dynasty, including 380 laws (written on 650 bamboo slips). This probably represents only a fraction of the entire law code. There is evidence here of a sophisticated legal tradition, with a nuanced sense of degrees of guilt and the severity of various crimes. One can imagine, however, popular resistance to the complicated categories and the strict penalties that included fines, mutilations, and executions.

When five men commit robbery and the illicit profit is one cash or more, amputate their left foot and tattoo them and make them *cheng-dan* [convict laborers]. When they are not fully five men and what they rob exceeds 660 cash, tattoo them, slice off their nose and make them *cheng-dan*. In case the illicit profit is not fully 660 cash, down to 220 cash, tattoo them and make them *cheng-dan*; if it is not fully 220 cash, banish them.

A plots to send B to rob and kill a person; as his share he receives ten cash. Question: B is not yet [five] feet tall [that is, still a youth]; how is A to be sentenced? He is warranted to be executed and exposed.

In a fight one uses a needle, a long needle or an awl; if the needle, the long needle or the awl wound people, how is each of these cases to be sentenced? When this was done during an un-premeditated fight, this warrants a fine of two suits of armour; when with murderous intent, it warrants tattooing and being made a *cheng-dan*.

A husband, his wife and his children, in all five persons, together commit robbery; they are warranted to suffer mutilation and be made *cheng-dan*. Now A arrests them all and denounces them. Question: with how much is A warranted to be rewarded? Per person a reward of two ounces [of gold].

The woman A leaves her husband and absconds; the man B also unauthorizedly absconds. They become man and wife. A does not inform him of the circumstances; only after two years, when she has born children, she informs him of the circumstances. B thereupon does not repudiate her. They are caught. How are they to be sentenced? They warrant tattooing and being made a *cheng-dan* and a grain-pounder [female convict laborer] respectively.

Source: A.F.P. Hulsewé, *Remnants of Ch'in Law* (Leiden: E. J. Brill, 1985), pp. 120, 138, 142, 158, 168.

DOCUMENT 4
Li Si on the Burning of the Books (213 B.C.E.)

> *Li Si was one of the foremost proponents of Legalism at the court of the First Emperor. His forceful response to a proposal that the First Emperor restore feudalism by enfeoffing his relatives demonstrates some of the key features of his thought. Not only did he argue for centralization and uniformity, but he completely rejected the idea that the past should be a model for the present and suggested that the Emperor ruthlessly crush dissent by destroying all books of history, literature, and philosophy. Li's single-minded focus on power became legendary, as did the cruelty of the First Emperor, who took Li's advice and executed 460 of his court scholars when the burning of the books failed to stop criticisms of his rule.*

The First Emperor gave a feast in the Xianyang Palace. The seventy Erudites went forward to toast him. Their Supervisor, Zhou Qingchen, advanced to offer praise: "In former times, Qin's territory was no more than one-thousand *li* [a third of a mile] on a side. Thanks to Your Majesty's perspicacity and sagacity, Qin has pacified the lands within the seas and expelled the uncivilized tribes. Wherever the sun and the moon shine, the people are submissive. The lands of the feudal lords are made into commanderies and counties so that everyone is content and happy with his own life, and the calamity of war does not exist. This is to be handed down to ten-thousand generations. Since antiquity, none has attained the prestige and virtues of your Majesty.

The First Emperor was pleased.

The Erudite Chunyu Yue, a native of Qi, came forward and said, "I have learned that Yin [Shang] and Zhou, ruling as kings for more than one-thousand years, enfeoffed their sons, brothers and meritorious ministers to branch out as support for the court itself. Now Your Majesty possesses all within the seas, yet your sons and brothers are all ordinary men. If there were suddenly vassals like Tian Chang or the Six Ministers of Jin, without support from your branched-out vassals, who would come to your rescue? I have never heard that an affair can exist for long without following [the ways of] antiquity. Now Qingchen has gone even further to flatter you, thus to intensify Your Majesty's mistakes. He is no loyal vassal.

The First Emperor handed down his deliberation.

Li Si, the Chancellor, said: "The Five Emperors did not duplicate each other's ways of governing, and the Three Dynasties did not inherit them from one another, but each regulated the world by his own means. It was not that they opposed each other, but that the times were different. Now Your Majesty has founded this great enterprise and attained merit which will last for ten-thousand generations; this is surely not that which an ignorant Confucian can understand. Moreover, what Chunyu Yue spoke of were matters of the Three Dynasties. Why should they be worth imitating? In different times, the feudal lords struggled against each other, so that they attracted sojourning scholars with rich rewards. Now the world has been pacified and laws and ordinances come from one source. The common people when managing their households shall put effort in agriculture and labor, and gentlemen when managing their households learn the laws, ordinances and prohibitions. Now these masters do not learn from the modern but from the ancient, with which they criticize the present time and confuse the black-haired. The Chancellor, Your Subject, risks his life to say that formerly the world was divided and in disorder, and none was able to unify it, therefore the feudal lords rose to vie for hegemony at the same time. In their words, they all talked about the ancient, thereby regarding the present system as harmful, and elaborated empty words to confuse reality. Each cherished what he had acquired from private learning to criticize what the sovereign has established. Now the Emperor, having united and grasped the world, has discriminated between black and white and established a single authority. But they are partial to their own learning and join together to criticize the laws and teachings. Upon hearing an ordinance has been issued, each debates it according to his learning. In the court, they criticize it in their hearts; outside, they debate it on the streets. To discredit the ruler is a means to be famous, and to be inclined to opposition is a means of showing superiority. They lead their followers to fabricate slander. If things like this are not banned, then the ruler's power will be diminished above, and factions will form below. To ban them is appropriate. I would ask that you burn all the records in the Scribes' offices which are not Qin's. If not needed by the Office of the Erudites, all songs, documents, and writings of the hundred schools, which anyone in the world has ventured to keep, should be brought to the governors and commandants to be thrown together and burned. Anyone who ventures to discuss songs and documents will be executed in the marketplace. Those who use the ancient system to criticize the present will be executed together with their families. Officials who witness or know of this crime yet fail to prosecute it will have the same punishment as the criminals. Thirty days after the ordinance has been issued, anyone who has not burned his books will be tattooed and sentenced to hard labor. What are exempted are books of medicine, divination, and horticulture. If one desires to learn laws and ordinances, he should make legal officials his teacher."

The Emperor decreed: "We approve."

Source: From "The Basic Annals of the First Emperor of Qin," *Shiji*, ch. 6. Translated by William H. Nienhauser, Jr., et al., *The Grand Scribe's Records* (Bloomington: Indiana University Press, 1994), 1:146–148. Reprinted with permission of the publisher.

DOCUMENT 5
Chen She's Rebellion (209 B.C.E.)

Chen She seems to have been a rather ordinary man, though with extraordinary ambitions. By seizing an opportune moment, he made a lasting name for himself, even if his personal success was short-lived. Almost immediately after the events described here he proclaimed himself king of Chu, but was assassinated six months later by his chariot driver. Although Chen She's was the first and best known of the revolts at the end of the

Qin, there were undoubtedly many others. Something of the chaotic nature of the times can be glimpsed in Chen's shifting justifications for rebellion—at various times he urged his men to save their own skins, to fight
for relatively popular Qin figures, to restore the past glories of the feudal
kingdom of Chu, and to create a new aristocracy (with himself as king,
of course).

Chen Sheng, whose [formal] name was Chen She, was a native of
Yangcheng; Wu Guang, or Wu Shu, was from Yangxia. When Chen She
was young, he was working one day in the fields with the other hired
men. Suddenly he stopped his plowing and went and stood on a hillock,
wearing a look of profound discontent. After a long while he announced,
"If I become rich and famous, I will not forget the rest of you!"

The other farm hands laughed and answered, "You are nothing but a
hired laborer. How could you ever become rich and famous?

Chen She gave a great sigh. "Oh, well," he said, "how could you little sparrows be expected to understand the ambitions of a swan?"

During the first year of the Second Emperor of Qin [209], in the seventh month, an order came for a force of 900 men from the poor side of
the town to be sent to garrison Yuyang. Chen She and Wu Guang were
among those whose turn it was to go, and they were appointed heads of
the levy of men. When the group had gone as far as Daze County, they
encountered such heavy rain that the road became impassable. It was apparent that the men would be unable to reach the appointed place on
time, an offence punishable by death. Chen She and Wu Guang ac-
cordingly began to plot together. "As things stand, we face death whether
we stay or run away," they said, "while if we were to start a revolt we
would likewise face death. Since we must die in any case, would it not
be better to die fighting for our country?"

"The world has long suffered under Qin," said Chen She. "From what
I have heard, the Second Emperor was a younger son and ought never
to have succeeded to the throne. The one who should have been made
ruler was Prince Fusu. But because Fusu several times remonstrated with
the former emperor, he was sent to lead the armies in the field. Someone has told me that, though Fusu was guilty of no crime, he has been
murdered by the Second Emperor. The common people have heard much
of Fusu's worth, but they do not know that he is dead. Xiang Yan was a
general of Chu who many times distinguished himself in battle. He took

good care of his troops and the people of Chu thought fondly of him. Some say that he is dead, but others say that he is only in hiding. Now with the group we have, if we could deceive people into thinking that I am Fusu and you are Xiang Yan, we could lead the world in our own tune, and there are sure to be many who will join in the chorus!"

Wu Guang approved of this idea, and they went to consult a diviner. The diviner guessed what the two were planning, and replied, "Your undertakings will all meet with success. But might you not seek your fortune with the spirits?"

Chen She and Wu Guang were delighted with the idea of enlisting supernatural aid in their scheme. "It must mean that we should first do something to overawe the men in our group!" they declared, and proceeded to write with cinnabar on a piece of silk: "Chen She shall be a king." They stuffed the silk into the belly of a fish someone had caught in a net. When one of the soldiers bought the fish and boiled it for his dinner, he discovered the message in the fish's belly and was greatly astonished. Also Chen She secretly sent Wu Guang to a grove of trees surrounding a shrine which was close to where the men were making camp. When night fell, Wu Guang lit a torch and, partly concealing it under a basket, began to wail like a fox and cry, "Great Chu shall rise again! Chen She shall be a king!"

The soldiers were filled with alarm, and when dawn came they talked here and there among themselves, pointing and staring at Chen Shu.

Wu Guang had always been kind to others and many of the soldiers would do anything for him. When the officer in command of the group was drunk, Wu Guang made a point of openly announcing several times that he was going to run away. In this way, Wu Guang hoped to arouse the commander's anger, get him to punish him, and so stir up the men's ire and resentment. As Wu Guang had expected, the commander began to beat him, when the commander's sword slipped out of its scabbard. Wu Guang sprang up, seized the sword, and killed the commander, Chen Shu rushed to his assistance and they proceeded to kill the other two commanding officers as well. Then they called together all the men of the group and announced: "Because of the rain we encountered, we cannot reach our rendezvous on time. And anyone who misses a rendezvous has his head cut off! Even if you should somehow escape with your heads, six or seven out of every ten of you are bound to die in the course of garrison duty. Now my brave fellows, if you are unwilling to die, we have nothing more to say. But if you would risk death then let us risk it for the sake of fame and glory! Kings and nobles, generals and ministers—such men are made, not born!"

The men of the garrison all replied, "We'll do whatever you say!" Then, in order to win the loyalty of the people, Chen She and Wu Guang falsely proclaimed themselves to be Prince Fusu and Xiang Yan. Baring their right shoulders, they raised the cry of "Great Chu!" and built an altar and swore an oath before it, offering as a sacrifice the heads of the commanding officers. Chen She set himself up as commander of the army, with Wu Guang as his colonel, and together they attacked Daze County. After capturing Daze County, they proceeded to attack and capture Qi. They dispatched Ge Ying, a man of Fuli, with a force to seize control of the area east of Qi, while they themselves attacked [the counties of] Zhi, Zan, Ku, Zhe, and Qiao, all of which submitted. Recruiting soldiers as they went along, they were able by the time they reached the city of Chen to build up a force of 600 or 700 chariots, over 1,000 horsemen, and 20,000 or 30,000 infantry.

Source: From the "Hereditary House of Chen She," *Shiji*, ch. 48. Translated by Burton Watson, *Records of the Grand Historian: Han Dynasty*, rev. ed. (New York and Hong Kong: *Renditions*-Columbia University Press, 1993), 1:1–3. Reprinted with permission of the publisher.

DOCUMENT 6
Liu Bang takes the Qin Capital (207 B.C.E.)

This account of Liu Bang's conquest of the Qin capital is remarkable for its emphasis on his kindness and repudiation of Legalist methods. With such behavior, he gained the support of the people, though his actions were not entirely altruistic. There was a certain measure of self-interest involved, and indeed, his sealing up of the treasures and palaces allowed him to later claim that he had simply been holding the capital for Xiang Yu. Xiang arrived a short time later with many more troops and would have killed his rival had Liu allowed his men to plunder the city. That job was left for Xiang Yu's army and Xiang was bitterly hated as a result. Liu, of course, eventually displaced Xiang Yu and became emperor of the Han Empire. When he did so, he put in place an elaborate law code based on Qin models, despite his promise in the speech that follows.

In the tenth month of the first year of Han [207], the troops of the Magistrate of Pei [Liu Bang] were in the end the first among the feudal lords to reach Bashang [a plain on the outskirts of the Qin capital]. The Qin king, Ziying, came riding in a white chariot harnessed with white horses, a cord tied around his neck, and holding the seals, tallies and caducei [scepter] of the august emperor, to surrender near the Zhi Road pavilion. Among the generals some spoke of executing the King of Qin. The Magistrate of Pei said, "When King Huai [the new king of Chu] first sent me, he originally considered that I would be able to be lenient; moreover, the man has already submitted in surrender; to go further and kill him would bring bad luck." Then he entrusted the King of Qin to his officers and finally headed west to enter Xianyang [the Qin capital]. He intended to stop and rest in the palaces, but Fan Kuai and Zhang Liang admonished him, and he sealed up the storehouses of treasure and wealth and returned to camp at Bashang. He summoned all the elders and prominent men from the local counties and said, "You elders have long suffered under Qin's harsh laws. Those who criticized the government were exterminated with their three kindred. Those who gathered to discuss the *Songs* and the *Documents* were executed and had their bodies exposed in the marketplace. I should be the king of the Land within the Passes, since I have agreed with the feudal lords that whoever enters the Pass first should rule over it as king. I will come to an agreement with you elders that there will be a legal code with only three articles: those who kill a person must die, those who injure a person and steal will be punished according to the offense. I will do away with all the rest of Qin's laws. All the officers and people will live in peace as before. Do not be afraid—I have come to do away with that which causes you elders harm, not to impose tyranny! The reason I have returned my army to Bashang is to await the arrival of the feudal lords and to reach a decision on the agreement." Then he sent men together with the Qin government officers to make rounds of inspection in the counties, districts and towns, and proclaim these things. The people of Qin were greatly pleased and strove to bring oxen, sheep, wine, and food to feast the officers in his army. The Magistrate of Pei refused to accept them, saying, "The grain in the granaries is plentiful, there is nothing we lack and I do not want to cause the people expense." The people were even more pleased and only feared that the Magistrate of Pei would not become King of Qin.

Source: From the "Basic Annals of Gaozu [Liu Bang]," *Shiji,* ch. 8. Translated by William H. Nienhauser, Jr., et al., *The Grand Scribe's Records* (Bloomington: Indiana University Press, 2002), 2:37–39. Reprinted with permission of the publisher.

DOCUMENT 7
Han Xin's advice to Liu Bang (206 B.C.E.)

This passage offers a fairly typical example of the way advisers attempted to persuade rulers to adopt a specific course of action. Liu Bang was particularly astute in choosing capable officers, heeding their counsel, and winning their loyalty. Xiang Yu, by contrast, had a more difficult time rewarding his followers and recognizing good advice. Han Xin had joined the rebellion in its early years but had gained no prominence because no one was willing to take him seriously. After Xiang Yu had gained control of China and assigned kingdoms, Liu Bang's minister Xiao He urged him to listen to Han Xin and demonstrate his trust in this relatively unknown strategist by making him a major general. A formal ceremony of promotion was announced, without revealing who the fortunate recipient would be.

The king [Liu Bang] gave his consent to this. All of the generals were filled with joy, each considering that it was himself who was about to be made a major general. But when the title was conferred, to the astonishment of the entire army, it was upon Han Xin. After the ceremony of investiture was concluded and Han Xin had returned to his seat, the king said, "Prime Minister Xiao He has often spoken to me about you, general. What sort of strategy is it that you would teach me?"

Han Xin expressed his gratitude for the honor and took advantage of the king's inquiry to ask a question of his own. "Anyone who marched east to contend for the empire would have to face Xiang Yu, would he not?"

"He would," replied the king.

"In Your Majesty's estimation, which of you, Xiang Yu or yourself, excels in fierceness of courage and depth of kindness?"

The king of Han was silent for a while and then he said, "I am inferior to Xiang Yu."

Han Xin bowed once more and commended the king, saying, "Yes, I too believe that you are inferior. But I once served Xiang Yu, and I would like to tell you what sort of person he is. When Xiang Yu rages and bellows it is enough to make a thousand men fall down in terror. But since he is incapable of employing wise generals, all of it amounts to no more than the daring of an ordinary man.

"When Xiang Yu meets people he is courteous and thoughtful, his manner of speaking is gentle and, if someone is ill or in distress, he will weep over him and give him his own food and drink. But when someone he has sent upon a mission has achieved merit and deserves to be honored and enfeoffed he will fiddle with the seal of investiture until it crumbles in his hand before he can bring himself to present it to the man. This sort of kindness deserves to be called merely womanish!

"Now although Xiang Yu has made himself dictator of the world and subjugated the other nobles to his rule, he has not taken up residence in the area within the Pass, but has made his capital of Pengcheng. He has gone against the agreement made with the Righteous Emperor [the former King Huai of Chu, whom Xiang will later have assassinated] and instead has given out kingdoms to the nobles on the basis on his own likes and preferences, which has resulted in much injustice. The nobles, seeing that Xiang Yu has banished the Righteous Emperor and sent him to reside in Jiangnan, when they return to their own territories in like manner drive out their sovereigns and make themselves rulers of the choicest lands. Xiang Yu has left death and destruction everywhere he has passed. Much of the world hates him. The common people do not submit to him out of affection, but are awed by his might alone. In name he is a dictator, but in truth he has lost the hearts of the world. Therefore I say that his might can be easily weakened!

"Now if you could only pursue the opposite policy and make use of the brave men of the world, what enemy would not fall before you? If you were to enfeoff your worthy followers with the territories of the empire, who would not submit? If you were to take your soldiers of righteousness and lead them back east where they long to return, who would not flee from your path?

"The three kings of the region of Qin were formerly generals of Qin and led the sons of Qin for several years. The number of men who were killed under their command exceeds estimation. In addition they deceived their men into surrendering to the other nobles and, when they reached Xin'an, Xiang Yu treacherously butchered over 200,000 soldiers of the Qin army who had surrendered, sparing only the three generals Zhang Han, Sima Xin, and Dong Yi. Therefore the fathers of Qin loath these three men with a passion that eats into their very bones. Now Xiang Yu has managed by sheer force to make kings of these men, but the people of Qin have no love for them. When you entered the Wu Pass, you inflicted not a particle of harm, but repealed the harsh laws of Qin and gave to the people a simple code of laws in three articles only, and there were none of the people of Qin who did not wish to make you their king. According to the agreement concluded among all the nobles, you ought to have been made king of the area within the Pass, and the people of the area all knew this. And when you were deprived of your rightful position and retired to the region of Han, the people of Qin were all filled with resentment. Now if you will raise your army and march east, you can win over the three kingdoms of Qin simply by proclamation!"

The king of Han was overjoyed and only regretted that he had been so long in discovering Han Xin. He proceeded to follow the strategy Han Xin had outlined and assigned to his generals the areas which each was to attack. In the eighth month the king of Han raised his army, marched east out of Chencang, and subjugated the three kingdoms of Qin.

Source: From the "Biography of the Marquis of Huaiyin [Han Xin]," *Shiji*, ch. 92. Translated by Burton Watson, *Records of the Grand Historian: Han Dynasty*, rev. ed. (New York and Hong Kong: *Renditions*-Columbia University Press, 1993), 1:165–167. Reprinted with permission of the publisher.

DOCUMENT 8
Liu Bang Becomes Emperor (202 B.C.E.)

This account of the day when Liu Bang took the title of emperor is from the Han shu, *which provides more detail than Sima Qian originally did in the* Shiji. *Liu is exhibiting admirable humility by professing reluctance and claiming to be "of little virtue"; a show of deference was an important part of moral justification for his rule. It is significant that the instigators of this promotion were the new aristocracy—men who had just been granted kingdoms—rather than officials or bureaucrats. If their motive was to strengthen their own claims by elevating the man who had granted them royal station, their trust was misplaced. By 195, when Liu*

Bang died, all but one of the new kings had been deposed and replaced by sons or brothers of Liu Bang.

The nobles sent up a petition to the King of Han [Liu Bang], saying: "The King of Chu, Han Xin; the King of Hann, Hann Xin; the King of Huainan, Qing Bu; the King of Liang, Peng Yue; the former King of Hengshan, Wu Rui; the King of Zhao, Zhang Ao; and the King of Yan, Zang Tu, risking death and making repeated obeisances, say to your Majesty the great King: In times past the Qin dynasty acted contrary to principle and the world punished it. You, great King, were the first to capture the King of Qin and subjugate Guanzhong [the land between the passes]—your achievements have been the greatest in the world. You have preserved the perishing and given repose to those in danger; you have rescued those who were ruined and have continued broken lines of descent in order to tranquilize all the people. Your achievements are abundant and your virtue is great. You have moreover granted favors to the vassal kings who have merit, enabling them to succeed in setting up their gods of the soil and grains. The division of the land has already been settled, but positions and titles are still confounded with one another, without the proper division of the superior from the inferior, so that the manifestation of your, the great King's, merits and virtue is not proclaimed to later generations. Risking death and making repeated obeisances, we offer to our superior the honorable title of Emperor."

The King of Han replied, "I, a person of little virtue, have heard that the title of emperor should be possessed by a man eminent in talent and virtue. An empty name without possessing its reality should not be adopted. Now you, vassal kings, have all highly exalted me, a person of little virtue. How could I therefore occupy such a position?"

The vassal kings all said, "You, great King, arose from small beginnings; you destroyed the seditious dynasty of Qin; your majesty stirs everything within the seas; moreover, starting from a secluded and mean region, from Hanzhong, you acted out your majesty and virtue, executing the unrighteous, setting up the meritorious, tranquilizing and establishing the empire. Meritorious officials all received territory and the income of towns; you did not appropriate them for yourself. Your virtue, great King, has been bestowed even to the borders of the four seas. We, vassal kings, find our speech inadequate to express it. For you to take the position of Emperor would be most appropriate. We hope that you, great King, will favor the world by doing so."

The King of Han replied, "Since the vassal kings would be favored by it and since they consider it to be an advantage to all the people in the world, it may be done." . . .

In the second month, on the day *jiawu* [Feb. 28] they presented to their superior the honorable title of Emperor, and the King of Han ascended the imperial throne upon the northern bank of the river Si.

Source: From the "Annals of Gaozu," *Han shu*, ch. 1B. Translated by Homer H. Dubs, *The History of the Former Han Dynasty* (Baltimore: Waverly Press, 1938), 1:99–102. Reprinted with permission of the American Council of Learned Societies.

DOCUMENT 9
Jia Yi on the Collapse of the Qin Empire (c. 180 B.C.E.)

Jia Yi (201–169) was a brilliant young scholar at the court of Emperor Wen. At that fairly early period in the Han dynasty, when the Liu family was still facing the threat of major rebellions, there was a great deal of interest in exactly how empires were won and lost. In particular, Han rulers wanted to avoid repeating the mistakes of the Qin, whatever those might have been. Jia wrote a famous essay asserting that Qin's political disaster was the result of moral failings, especially the harsh policies that had alienated the common people. In making this argument, he was advancing ideals of government that had been proposed by Confucius long before.

After the First Emperor of Qin had united the lands within the seas, absorbed the territories of the feudal lords, and faced south to proclaim himself emperor and shepherd the people within the four seas, the intellectuals of the world gracefully turned toward his teaching. Why did they do so? The answer is there had been no true king for a long time in recent history. When the Zhou court declined and the Five Hegemons died, orders could not be carried out throughout the world. Thus the feudal lords strove to campaign against each other, the strong invading the weak, the many violating the few, military forces never rested and both intellectuals and commoners exhausted and worn out. Then, when the First Emperor of Qin faced south on the throne to rule the world as king, this meant there was a Son of Heaven above. Since the multitude of people were longing to settle down to a peaceful life, everyone gave up his preoccupations to look up to the sovereign. Just at this time, the First Emperor could keep his prestige and secure his merit. The basis of stability or instability lay in this.

The First Emperor of Qin, harboring an avaricious heart and following a self-assertive mind, not trusting his meritorious vassals or keeping close to intellectuals and commoners, abolished the kingly way of ruling, established his personal authority, banned writings and books, stiffened punitive laws, promoted craft and power, neglected benevolence and righteousness, and made tyranny the first rule of the world. The fact is, those unifying the world esteem craft and power, those settling the world value compliance and convenience. This is to say that acquisition and conservation require different techniques. The First Emperor of Qin braved the Warring States period to rule the world as king. His way of rule did not change, his policy did not alter. This means the ways he acquired and conserved the world were not different. He isolated himself to possess it, therefore his demise was waiting around the corner. Given that the First Emperor of Qin had taken into consideration matters of his preceding generations in Qin as well as the history of Yin [Shang] and Zhou with which to design and execute his policies, even if there were licentious and arrogant rulers among his descendants, there would have been no calamity of subversion. Thus the way the Three Kings had founded the world made their names illustrious and their enterprises endure.

Then, when the Second Emperor was enthroned, everyone in the world stretched out his neck to look forward to his policies. The situation was such that those out in the cold would benefit even from coarse cloth, those in hunger would savor even dregs and bran. That the people of the world were thirsty was a resource for the new ruler. This means it is easy to be kind to troubled people. Formerly, if the Second Emperor had conducted himself even as a middling ruler and employed the loyal and the worthy, and if the ruler and the vassals had joined their minds to worry about the calamity of the people within the seas, mournfully corrected the mistakes of the Late Emperor, divided the territory and separated the people to enfeoff the descendants of the meritorious vassals, founded feudal states and invested their lords to show respect to the world, emptied the jails and prisons and exempted convicts from punishment or execution, eliminated implicating wives and children of convicts and other miscellaneous offenses and let each of those in detention return home, opened granaries and distributed wealth to relieve the orphaned, the childless, the poor and the destitute, lightened taxation and reduced labor projects to assist the people in need, simplified laws and lessened punishments to put people on probation, so that all the people in the world would be able to renew their lives, change their bearing, cultivate their conduct, and be prudent about themselves, and prevented the grievances of the myriad people, the world would have gathered behind him. If all the people within the four seas were contented and each found his lot peaceful and enjoyable, fearing nothing but drastic change, so that even if a deceitful man were to appear, the vassals would have had no means to ply their cleverness and insurrectionary treachery would have been stopped. The Second Emperor could not adopt this strategy, and even intensified the situation by his unreasonableness; ruining his ancestral temples and people, he renewed the building of the E-pang palace, increased punitive laws and stiffened punishments, made judicial rulings harsh and stern, awards and punishments improper, taxation limitless, the world full of labor projects, and officials unable to function. The common people were destitute and poor, yet the ruler would not take care of and relieve them.

This being the case, when treacherous and fraudulent elements later rose together, the superiors and inferiors in the government concealed facts from each other. Those being condemned were so numerous that those to be executed could be seen one after another on roads. The people of the world suffered for this. From the lord and ministers down to the multitudinous commoners, everyone harbored a sense of insecurity and found himself in a hopelessly miserable reality and none were able to have peace of mind in his position, therefore, the state could be easily shattered. Thus when Chen She, neither applying the worthiness of Kings Tang and Wu [founders of the Shang and Zhou dynasties], nor depending on the prestige of the nobles, raised his arms in revolt at Daze (Great Marsh), the world responded in accord; the reason for this was that the people felt in peril.

Source: From Jia Yi's essay "The Faults of Qin," appended by Sima Qian at the end of the "Basic Annals of the First Emperor of Qin," *Shiji*, ch. 6. Translated by William H. Nienhauser, Jr., et al., *The Grand Scribe's Records* (Bloomington: Indiana University Press, 1994), 1:168–169. Reprinted with permission of the publisher.

DOCUMENT 10
Excerpt from a Memorial by Chao Cuo on Agriculture
(178 B.C.E.)

In this memorial, Chao Cuo was trying to convince Emperor Wen to build up the agricultural base of the empire by reducing taxes and allowing peasants to use surplus grain to earn advances in rank and commute legal penalties. In addition, he argued that commercial activities should be discouraged by discriminating against merchants. Emperor Wen took this advice and his reign was remembered as one of peace, prosperity, and budget surpluses (especially when compared to the aggressive policies of Emperor Wu, which nearly bankrupted the dynasty). In the short excerpt below, there is undoubtedly some exaggeration of the hardships of farming, but it does offer a rough sketch of the lives of the common people.

Now in a peasant family of five members there are not less than two persons who render labor service. All that they can cultivate is not more than one hundred mu [11 acres]. The yield from one hundred mu is not more than one hundred piculs [670 pounds].

They till the land in spring, hoe in summer, harvest in autumn, and store in winter. Besides they have to cut wood for fuel, work in the government buildings, and render labor service. In the spring they cannot escape the wind and dust; in the summer they cannot escape the heat; in the autumn they cannot escape the chilling rain; and in the winter they cannot escape the cold. Throughout the four seasons they do not have a single day of rest. Furthermore, their private expenditures for parting with those who are leaving and for welcoming those who are coming, for consoling with the bereaved, visiting the sick, caring for the orphans, and bringing up the young, all have to be defrayed from that income. Although they are already so industrious and straightened, still they have to suffer from the calamities of flood and drought. Collections are urgent, taxation exorbitant; and the taxes are collected at no fixed date. Orders issued in the morning have to be executed in the evening. Those who have something sell it at half price; those who have nothing have to borrow at 100 percent interest. Hence, there are people who have sold their land, their houses, their wives and children in order to pay their debts (i.e., taxes).

Source: From the "Treatise on Food and Money," *Han shu*, ch. 24A. Translated by Cho-yun Hsu, *Han Agriculture* (Seattle: University of Washington Press, 1980), pp. 161–162.

DOCUMENT 11
Memorial from Chunyu Tiying to Emperor Wen (c. 176 B.C.E.)

The sort of informal power that women could have in the Han Empire is illustrated by this story from the Lienü zhuan *(Traditions of Exemplary Women), a collection of biographies that was compiled in the Han dynasty by Liu Xiang (79–8). Here a selfless young woman's eloquent petition both saves her father and furthers social justice for the empire as a whole.*

The "Daughter of the Director of the Great Granary of Qi," whose given name was Tiying, was the youngest daughter of the Great Granary Director Lord Chunyu (c. 216–150) of the Han dynasty. Lord Chunyu had no sons but five daughters.

During the reign of Emperor Wen the Filial (180–157) Lord Chunyu was convicted of a crime and faced punishment. At this time the government still utilized corporal punishment. According to imperial orders, Chunyu was fettered and sent to a prison in Chang'an [the capital]. On the way to Chang'an, Chunyu cursed his daughters saying, "I have children but no sons. In times of trouble they are utterly useless!" Tiying, for her part, wept bitterly and followed her father to Chang'an and memorialized the emperor, saying,

While your handmaiden's father served as an official, all the people of Qi praised him as upright and just. But now he has been tried in a court of law and faces punishment. I grieve that the dead will have no chance to live again and that those who undergo a mutilating punishment cannot be made whole again. Although they desire to reform and begin again, they have no way to do so. Please allow me to enter service as a palace slave to redeem my father's crime and so that he may make a new beginning.

The emperor received the memorial and, moved by her plea, he made the following proclamation:

> I have heard that in the time of [the legendary sovereign] Shun, he used insignia on robes and hats and other kinds of markings on clothing as a form of punishment and the people committed no crimes. Great indeed was his rule! Nowadays, however, the law prescribes the five forms of mutilating punishments, yet wrongdoing does not cease. Wherein lies the fault? It is due to my deficient virtue and failure to teach the people intelligently. I am deeply ashamed. When instruction is corrupt, the ignorant masses fall into crime. The *Book of Songs* says, "Our kind and courteous ruler, He is father and mother to his people." Nowadays, when a person has committed some fault, no instruction is proffered but he is punished straightaway. If someone wants to reform and do good, his way is obstructed. I pity such people greatly! Now, when punishments extend to severing limbs or cutting flesh, the victims must suffer an entire lifetime. How utterly cruel and injudicious! How indeed can we be called the father and mother of the people? Let the corporal punishments be abolished!"

After this incident, those who had previously been punished by drilling into the skull had their heads shaved, those who had been punished by having their ribs extracted were now caned, and those who had their feet cut off were now shackled. Lord Chunyu was therefore spared. The eulogy says, "Tiying pleaded her father's case with great wisdom. She drew upon her earnest intent and submitted a memorial that was both eloquent and concise. Though they were the words of a mere girl, she inspired her sovereign to abolish corporal punishments and to save her father."

Source: From the *Lienü zhuan* [Traditions of Exemplary Women] 6.15. Translated by Anne Behnke Kinney.

DOCUMENT 12
An Edict of Emperor Wen (163 B.C.E.)

*The following edict is a model of Confucian rulership. Ever concerned
for the welfare of the masses, the emperor, when faced with disturbing reports, first looks for faults within himself, then examines current social
practices, and finally asks his ministers to suggest reforms. The fact that
he believes that he might be responsible for even natural disasters shows
the increasing importance of ideas about the Mandate of Heaven, since
floods, droughts, and epidemics were viewed as evidence of Heaven's displeasure. As emperor, it was his responsibility to ensure balance and harmony throughout the cosmos, which included the three realms of Heaven,
Earth, and Man.*

Recently for many years there have continually been no good harvests.
Moreover there have been visitations of floods, droughts, sickness, and
epidemics. We have been very much worried because of them. We are
ignorant and not perspicacious and do not yet understand just what is to
blame. We have been thinking: is there some fault in Our way of government or is there some defect in Our conduct? Or is it that We have
not obeyed the Way of Heaven or have perhaps not obtained the advantages of Earth, or are the affairs of men in great discord, or have the
spirits and divinities been neglected so that they have not enjoyed Our
offerings? How has this been brought about? Or is it that the salaries of
the officials are perhaps too lavish, or that useless activities are perhaps
too many? How is it that the people's food is scarce and lacking?

Now when the fields are measured, they have not decreased, and when
the population is counted, it has not increased, so that the amount of
land per person is greater than in ancient times. Yet there is very much
too little food; where does the blame for it lie? Is it that Our subjects devote themselves to what is least important, whereby those persons who
injure agriculture are multiplied? Is it due to the fact that they make wine
and lees, thereby wasting much grain, and the masses of food are given
to the six kinds of domestic animals? I have not yet been able to attain
the proper mean between what is immaterial and what is important. Let
this matter be discussed with the Lieutenant Chancellor, the marquises,
the officials of ranks worth two thousand piculs, and the Erudites. Should
there be anything that might be of assistance to Our subjects, let them

apply themselves with all their minds and think deeply about the matter. Let them not hide anything from Us.

Source: From the "Annals of Emperor Wen," *Han shu*, ch. 4. Translated by Homer H. Dubs, *The History of the Former Han Dynasty* (Baltimore: Waverly Press, 1938), 1:261–262. Reprinted with permission of the American Council of Learned Societies.

DOCUMENT 13
Two Han Poems (c. 109 B.C.E.)

The two poems that follow offer perspectives on life in the Han Empire that differ from those of the educated males who wrote most of the records. The first is a poem attributed to Liu Xijun, the daughter of a Han king. After her father's unsuccessful rebellion and suicide, she was sent to be the bride of an elderly chieftain of the Wusun nomads. Her marriage was not a happy one, and she met with her husband, who could not understand her language, only once or twice a year. Later she was forced to marry his grandson. The poem describes her primitive living conditions and her homesickness, and it reveals a woman's view of the marriage politics that were part of the barbarian-relations policies of the Han. The second poem is an undated, anonymous folk song expressing the feelings of village elders as they sang and pounded the earth to keep time. For many in the empire, court politics must have seemed mostly irrelevant to their daily lives.

"Song of the Wusun Princess"

My family arranged a marriage for me, in this distant corner of the world,
Sent me to a foreign land, to the King of the Wusun.
A tent is my house, with felt for walls.
Meat is my only food and fermented mare's milk my drink.
I never stop longing for home, my heart never stops breaking,
Oh that I were a yellow crane, winging my way home.

"Earth-Pummeling Song"

We begin work when the sun comes up,
We rest when the sun goes down.

We drink when we dig wells,
Eat when we till the land.
What do we care about the might of the emperor!

Source: Translated by Anne Behnke Kinney.

DOCUMENT 14
Excerpt from the Debate on Salt and Iron (81 B.C.E.)

Emperor Wu's aggressive foreign policy—which brought many years of war against the Xiongnu nomads as well as peoples in Central Asia, Southwest China, and Korea—nearly bankrupted the treasury. To make up for budget shortfalls, his advisers put into place government monopolies of salt, iron, and liquor. There was also a program called the "equable marketing system," under which the government purchased grain when prices were low, and then sold it again when prices rose. After Emperor Wu's death, this sort of direct interference in the economy was criticized by Confucian scholars, and their arguments were recorded in the Debate on Salt and Iron. In general, they believed that commerce and industry were distractions from the primary occupation of farming, and they felt that the government was setting a bad example. Readers should probably be suspicious of the minister's argument that the ruler had only the welfare of the common people in mind, but modern students may also have doubts about the scholars' assertion that if only the emperor exhibited true Confucian virtue, he would have "no enemies anywhere" and the savage Xiongnu would "joyfully submit" to his authority. Though the current text of the debate shows the scholars winning at several points, government policy changed little as a result of these discussions.

In 81 an imperial edict directed the chancellor and chief minister to confer with a group of wise and learned men about the people's hardships.

The learned men responded: We have heard that the way to rule lies in preventing frivolity while encouraging morality, in suppressing the pursuit of profit while opening the way for benevolence and duty. When profit is not emphasized, civilization flourishes and the customs of the people improve.

Recently, a system of salt and iron monopolies, a liquor excise tax, and an equable marketing system have been established throughout the country. These represent financial competition with the people which undermines their native honesty and promotes selfishness. As a result, few among the people take up the fundamental pursuits [agriculture] while many flock to the secondary [trade and industry]. When artificiality thrives, simplicity declines; when the secondary flourishes, the basic decays. Stress on the secondary makes the people decadent; emphasis on the basic keeps them unsophisticated. When the people are unsophisticated, wealth abounds; when they are extravagant, cold and hunger ensue.

We desire that the salt, iron, and liquor monopolies and the system of equable marketing be abolished. In that way the basic pursuits will be encouraged, and the people will be deterred from entering secondary occupations. Agriculture will then greatly prosper. This would be expedient.

The minister: The Xiongnu rebel against our authority and frequently raid the frontier settlements. To guard against this requires the effort of the nation's soldiers. If we take no action, these attacks and raids will never cease. The late emperor [Emperor Wu] had sympathy for the long-suffering of the frontier settlers who live in fear of capture by the barbarians. As defensive measures, he therefore built forts and beacon relay stations and set up garrisons. When the revenue for the defense of the frontier fell short, he established the salt and iron monopolies, the liquor excise tax, and the system of equable marketing. Wealth increased and was used to furnish the frontier expenses.

Now our critics wish to abolish these measures. They would have the treasury depleted and the border deprived of funds for its defense. They would expose our soldiers who defend the frontier passes and walls to hunger and cold, since there is no other way to supply them. Abolition is not expedient.

The learned men: Confucius observed, "The ruler of a kingdom or head of a family does not worry about his people's being poor, only about their being unevenly distributed. He does not worry about their being few, only about their being dissatisfied." Thus, the emperor should not talk of much and little, nor the feudal lords of advantage and harm, nor the minister of gain and loss. Instead they all should set examples of benevolence and duty, and virtuously care for people, for then those nearby will flock to them and those faraway will joyfully submit to their authority. Indeed, the master conqueror need not fight, the expert warrior needs no soldiers, and the great commander need not array his troops.

If you foster high standards in the temple and courtroom, you need only make a bold show and bring home your troops, for the king who practices benevolent government has no enemies anywhere. What need can he then have for expense funds?

The minister: The Xiongnu are savage and cunning. They brazenly push through the frontier passes and harass the interior, killing provincial officials and military officers at the border. Although they have long deserved punishment for their lawless rebellion, Your Majesty has taken pity on the financial exigencies of the people and has not wished to expose his officers to the wilderness. Still, we cherish the goal of raising a great army and driving the Xiongnu back north.

I again assert that to do away with the salt and iron monopolies and equable marketing system would bring havoc to our frontier military policies and would be heartless toward those on the frontier. Therefore this proposal is inexpedient.

The learned men: The ancient honored the use of virtue and discredited the use of arms. Confucius said, "If the people of far-off lands do not submit, then the ruler must attract them by enhancing his refinement and virtue. When they have been attracted, he gives them peace."

At present, morality is discarded and reliance is placed on military force. Troops are raised for campaigns and garrisons are stationed for defense. It is the long-drawn-out campaigns and the ceaseless transportation of provisions that burden our people at home and cause our frontier soldiers to suffer from hunger and cold.

The establishment of the salt and iron monopolies and the appointment of financial officers to supply the army were meant to be temporary measures. Therefore, it is expedient that they now be abolished.

Source: From the *Yantie lun* (Debate on Salt and Iron), ch. 1. Translated by Patricia Buckley Ebrey, *Chinese Civilization: A Sourcebook*, 2nd ed. (New York: The Free Press, 1993), pp. 60–62. Reprinted with the permission of The Free Press, a Division of Simon & Schuster Adult Publishing Group. Copyright © 1993 by Patricia Buckley Ebrey. All rights reserved.

GLOSSARY

Bureaucracy: Government by salaried, professional administrators who could be hired and fired by the ruler at will. The term usually implies the specialization of government functions into different bureaus or departments.

Censorate: The branch of government that audited and reported on the performance of officials in the civil and military branches.

Chancellor: The head of the civil branch of government.

Commandery: An administrative unit in the Qin and Han empires similar to a province. Commanderies were administered by centrally appointed, nonhereditary officials.

Confucian Classics: Five texts traditionally thought to have been edited by Confucius—the *Book of Documents*, the *Book of Songs*, the *Record of Ritual*, the *Classic of Changes*, and the *Spring and Autumn Annals*.

Confucianism: A philosophical school associated with Confucius, which focused on literary and historical writings from pre-imperial China and the humane ethics found in such texts. Han Confucianism combined Confucius' original teachings with proto-scientific ideas such as yin/yang and the Five Phases.

Daoism: A philosophical school associated with Laozi, which takes the Dao, or the Way, as its model. Daoist thinkers praised nature and non-action, and emphasized that many value judgments were relative or subjective.

Dowager empress: The emperor's mother.

Dowry: Money given by a woman's family to their daughter when she married. Since a Chinese bride became part of her husband's extended family, her new relatives at times claimed that money as their own.

Dynasty: A period when one particular family line is in power.

Enfeoff: To grant land as part of a feudal relationship.

Erudite: An official post in the Qin and Han periods for classically trained scholars who served as imperial advisers. They often provided the emperor with historical precedents for (and against) imperial policy.

Feudalism: A decentralized governmental system in which a ruler grants nobles land, as well as the right to tax and conscript the local population, in return for loyalty and a promise of continuing military service. The ruler then has little control over what happens within that territory, which is run by the local lord as he sees fit.

Filial piety: Respect and obedience to one's parents; thought of as the highest moral virtue in early China.

Five Phases: A theory of change by which five phases—Fire, Water, Earth, Wood, and Metal—replaced each other and exerted a dominant influence over all phenomena in sequential fashion. All natural and social phenomena were correlated with particular phases.

Hegemon: A military leader who, in China, kept order on behalf of a king (though in actuality he was often more powerful than the king) or who was first among equals within a group of kings. Xiang Yu rejected the Qin title of "emperor" and combined these two roles when he proclaimed himself a "hegemon-king."

Inner court: The empress, concubines, and eunuchs who lived in the inner quarters of the imperial palace and exercised informal influence on imperial policies.

Legalism: A philosophical school that recommended that the affairs of state be run according to impartial laws and the standardized use of punishments and rewards. Often noted for their ruthlessness, its adherents cared less for tradition and morality than for efficiency and control.

Mandate of Heaven: Heaven's authorization of a dynasty to rule over China. It was thought that Heaven (an impersonal spiritual force) conferred this power in recognition of a ruler's virtue and continued to support his descendants as long as they ruled in accordance with the dictates of Heaven. If a king or an emperor became corrupt and oppressive, Heaven withdrew its mandate and gave it to another more worthy man, who would then be justified in leading a rebellion.

Primogeniture: A pattern of inheritance in which the oldest son of the primary wife received all of the family's wealth, lands, and titles.

Sericulture: The production of silk from the care and feeding of silkworms to the weaving of the finished product.

Yin/yang: Two opposing forces that make up the natural world. Yin is associated with concepts such as femininity, completion, cold, darkness, and earth. Yang is associated with masculinity, creation, heat, light, and heaven. According to some thinkers, these two forces are complementary and should ideally be in balance. Other scholars envisioned them as hierarchically based, so that one was superior and the other inferior.

ANNOTATED BIBLIOGRAPHY

Books

General Background

De Bary, Theodore, and Irene Bloom, eds. *Sources of Chinese Tradition: From Earliest Times to 1600.* 2nd ed. New York: Columbia University Press, 1999. A collection of translated documents from ancient and imperial China, with an emphasis on philosophy and intellectual history.

Ebrey, Patricia Buckley. *The Cambridge Illustrated History of China.* Cambridge: Cambridge University Press, 1996. A good general overview of all of Chinese history, with exceptional maps and photos.

Hansen, Valerie. *The Open Empire: A History of China to 1600.* New York: Norton, 2000. A college textbook on early China. Hansen's book is well written and filled with intriguing details about everyday life.

Murowchick, Robert E., ed. *China: Ancient Culture, Modern Land.* Cradles of Civilization Series. Norman: University of Oklahoma Press, 1994. Lavish illustrations accompany this relatively brief recounting of ancient Chinese history. Chapters are written by recognized experts.

Temple, Robert. *The Genius of China: 3,000 Years of Science, Discovery, and Invention.* New York: Simon & Schuster, 1986. This introduction to Chinese science and technology distills some of the most important points from Joseph Needham's massive series *Science and Civilization in China.*

Specialized Studies of Early China

Birrell, Anne. *Popular Songs and Ballads of Han China.* Honolulu: University of Hawaii Press, 1993. Birrell's translations and discussions of poems from the Han period offer insight into the inner lives of people of the time, with chapters devoted to fables, antiwar ballads, love songs, and more.

Bodde, Derk. *China's First Unifier: A Study of Ch'in Dynasty Life as Seen in the Life of Li Ssu.* Hong Kong: Hong Kong University Press, 1967. An excellent study of the Qin dynasty.

Ch'ü T'ung-tsu. *Han Social Structure.* Edited by Jack L. Dull. Seattle: University of Washington Press, 1972. A careful analysis of the role of family, women, marriage, and social class in Han times. The second half of the book consists of annotated translations of relevant passages from the *Shiji*, the *Han shu*, and the *Hou Han shu* (History of the Later Han Dynasty).

Cook, Constance A., and John S. Major, eds. *Defining Chu: Image and Reality in Ancient China.* Honolulu: University of Hawaii Press, 1999. A collection of essays examining the culture of South China in early times.

Cotterell, Arthur. *The First Emperor of China: The Greatest Archeological Find of Our Time.* New York: Holt, Rinehart and Winston, 1981. More than just an enthusiastic report of the terra-cotta army, this book includes chapters on the historical context of Qin China and biographies of the First Emperor and Li Si.

Durrant, Stephen W. *The Cloudy Mirror: Tension and Conflict in the Writings of Sima Qian.* Albany: State University of New York Press, 1995. A literary introduction to the *Shiji* that explores the relationship between Sima Qian's life and the history he wrote.

Graham, A. C. *Disputers of the Tao: Philosophical Argument in Ancient China.* La Salle, IL: Open Court, 1989. There are many general introductions to Chinese philosophy, but this is one of the most accurate and accessible, written by a pioneer in the field.

Hardy, Grant. *Worlds of Bronze and Bamboo: Sima Qian's Conquest of History.* New York: Columbia University Press, 1999. An analysis of the unusual structure of Sima Qian's history, with observations on how Sima Qian's view of history differs from classic historians of Greece and Rome.

Hinsch, Bret. *Women in Early Imperial China.* Lanham, MD: Rowman & Littlefield, 2002. Various aspects of the lives of women in the Qin and Han dynasties are explored in this very useful overview.

Hsu, Cho-yun. *Han Agriculture: The Formation of Early Chinese Agrarian Economy.* Edited by Jack L. Dull. Seattle: University of Washington Press, 1980. A survey of agricultural practices in the Han; the second half of the book consists of translated excerpts from the *Shiji*, the *Han shu*, and the *Hou Han shu*.

Hulsewé, A.F.P. *Remnants of Han Law*. Leiden: E. J. Brill, 1955. A detailed study of the legal system of the Han Empire, with a translation of *Han shu 23*: "The Treatise on Punishments and Laws."

Kern, Martin. *The Stele Inscriptions of Ch'in Shih-Huang: Text and Ritual in Early Chinese Imperial Representation*. New Haven: American Oriental Society, 2000. Kern offers a striking new interpretation of the Qin regime, in addition to a careful study and translation of the inscriptions of the First Emperor.

Kinney, Anne Behnke. *Representations of Childhood and Youth in Early China*. Stanford: Stanford University Press, 2003. An examination of the idea of childhood in early China, from the perspective of Chinese cosmology, medicine, law, statecraft, and dynastic history.

Lewis, Mark Edward. *Sanctioned Violence in Early China*. Albany: State University of New York Press, 1990. Though his arguments can be somewhat technical, Lewis carefully analyzes evidence from early China on the social and political shifts of the Warring States Era, a time when aristocratic warfare gave way to armies conscripted from the masses.

———. *Writing and Authority in Early China*. Albany: State University of New York Press, 1999. An analysis of intellectual currents and the role of writing in the early Chinese state.

Li Xueqin. *Eastern Zhou and Qin Civilizations*. Translated by K. C. Chang. New Haven: Yale University Press, 1985. A scholarly review of archaeological discoveries from the late Zhou and Qin dynasties.

Loewe, Michael. *A Biographical Dictionary of the Qin, Former Han, and Xin Periods (221 B.C.–A.D. 24)*. Leiden: E. J. Brill, 2000. An astonishing work of scholarship that brings together information about everyone mentioned in the standard histories for the Qin and Former Han dynasties. It also includes detailed maps and information on official titles and administrative units.

———. *Chinese Ideas of Life and Death: Faith and Reason in the Han Period (202 B.C.–A.D. 220*. London: George Allen and Unwin, 1982. An overview of beliefs dominant in the Han period, including those associated with religion, nature, and government.

———. *Crisis and Conflict in Han China*. London: Allen and Unwin, 1974. A study of the major intellectual, political, and historical events of the Former Han dynasty.

———. *Everyday Life in Early Imperial China*. New York: Dorset, 1968. Comprehensive account of life in the Han dynasty, from farmers to soldiers to merchants and artisans to government officials.

Loewe, Michael, and Edward L. Shaughnessy, eds. *The Cambridge History of Ancient China: From the Origins of Civilization to 221 B.C.* New York: Cambridge University Press, 1999. An authoritative synthesis of scholarship on pre-imperial China, written by world-renowned experts. The use of archaeological evidence is particularly noteworthy.

Major, John. *Heaven and Earth in Early Han Thought: Chapters Three, Four, and Five of the 'Huainanzi.'* Albany: State University of New York Press, 1993. A study of cosmological thought in the Han.

Nylan, Michael. *The Five 'Confucian' Classics.* New Haven: Yale University Press, 2001. An introduction to the history and contents of the Five Classics.

Peerenboom, R. P. *Law and Morality in Ancient China: The Silk Manuscripts of Huang-Lao.* Albany: State University of New York Press, 1993. A study of law in early China based on recently discovered manuscripts.

Pirazzoli-t'Serstevens, Michèle. *The Han Dynasty.* Translated by Janet Seligman. New York: Rizzoli, 1982. Part art book, part history book, this volume covers the main aspects of history and culture in the Han Empire, with numerous full-color photographs.

Queen, Sarah A. *From Chronicle to Canon: The Hermeneutics of the Spring and Autumn according to Tung Chung-shu.* Cambridge: Cambridge University Press, 1996. A detailed analysis of the life and thought of Dong Zhongshu.

Raphals, Lisa. *Sharing the Light: Representations of Women and Virtue in Early China.* Albany: State University of New York Press, 1998. This book examines issues central to women's status in early China.

Roth, Harold D. *Original Tao: Inward Training and the Foundations of Taoist Mysticism.* New York: Columbia University Press, 1999. This study examines Daoism in the early Han.

Sinor, Denis, ed. *The Cambridge History of Early Inner Asia.* New York: Cambridge University Press, 1990. As with the other Cambridge Histories, this collection of essays offers first-rate scholarship on a wide range of topics from the Scythians and the Huns to the Turks and Tibetans. The treatment of nomadic peoples that border China (especially the Xiongnu [or Hsiung-nu]) offers significant insights for Chinese history.

Twitchett, Denis, and Michael Loewe, eds. *The Cambridge History of China, Vol. 1: The Ch'in and Han Empires 221 B.C.–A.D. 220.* New York: Cambridge University Press, 1986. The best survey of the Qin and Han dynasties available, with comprehensive and authoritative chapters on political history, intellectual history, economic history, and social history.

Unschuld, Paul U. *Medicine in China: A History of Ideas.* Berkeley: University of California Press, 1985. A survey of medicine in China, from earliest times through the Han.

Vankeerberghen, Griet. *The Huainanzi and Liu An's Claim to Moral Authority.* Albany: State University of New York Press, 2001. A study of an important philosophical text in the Han dynasty and the kingdom in which it was written.

Wang Zhongshu. *Han Civilization.* Translated by K. C. Chang and collaborators. New Haven: Yale University Press, 1982. A scholarly review of archaeological finds from the Han Empire.

Watson, Burton. *Ssu-ma Ch'ien, Grand Historian of China.* New York: Columbia University Press, 1958. The groundbreaking work in English on Sima Qian. It includes a translation of *Shiji,* ch. 130, the historian's autobiography.

Welch, Holmes, and Anna Seidel, eds. *Facets of Taoism: Essays in Chinese Religion.* New Haven: Yale University Press, 1979. This collection of papers from an International Conference on Daoism in 1972 provided the English-speaking world with one of its first glimpses of specialized topics in Daoist studies from throughout Chinese history. Many of the articles are still well-worth reading as an introduction to various Daoist figures and movements.

Wilbur, C. Martin. *Slavery in Han China.* New York: Russell and Russell, 1943. Still the authoritative account on an important and often overlooked topic in ancient China.

Yang, Xiaoneng, ed. *The Golden Age of Chinese Archaeology: Celebrated Discoveries from the People's Republic of China.* New Haven: Yale University Press, 1999. A gallery guide for a touring museum exhibition. Full-page, full-color photographs of some of the most famous artifacts from early China.

Yates, Robin D. S. *Five Lost Classics: Tao, Huang-Lao, and Yin-Yang in Han China.* New York: Ballantine Books, 1997. A translation and study of recently excavated texts concerning correlative cosmology from early China.

Translations

Ban Gu. *Han shu* (c. 100 C.E.).

- Homer H. Dubs, trans. *The History of the Former Han Dynasty.* 3 vols. Baltimore, MD: Waverly, 1938–1955. This is an annotated translation of the first twelve (out of one hundred) chapters, which are the basic annals of the early Han emperors.

- Burton Watson, trans. *Court and Courier in Han China*. New York: Columbia University Press, 1974. A translation of ten of the most interesting chapters of the *Han shu*, including the lives of imperial princes, court ladies, generals, officials, wandering knights, and a court jester.

Confucius. *Analects* (fifth century B.C.E.). Three recommended translations:

- D. C. Lau, trans. *Confucius: The Analects*. New York: Penguin, 1979.
- Simon Leys, trans. *The Analects of Confucius*. New York: W. W. Norton, 1997.
- Authur Waley, trans. *The Analects of Confucius*. New York: Vintage Books, 1938.

Gale, Esson M., trans. *Discourses on Salt and Iron: A Debate on State Control of Commerce and Industry in Ancient China*. Leiden: E. J. Brill, 1931. An annotated translation of chapters 1–19 of the *Yantie lun*, the record of the debate in 81 B.C.E. on the salt and iron monopolies.

Han Feizi. *Han Feizi* (third century B.C.E.).

- W. K. Liao, trans. *The Complete Works of Han Fei Tzu: A Classic of Chinese Legalism*. 2 vols. London: A. Probsthain, 1939 (vol. 1) and 1959 (vol. 2).
- Burton Watson, trans. *Han Fei Tzu: Basic Writings*. New York: Columbia University Press, 1964.

Hulsewé, A.F.P. *Remnants of Ch'in Law*. Leiden: E. J. Brill, 1985. Scholarly, annotated translation of the Qin legal documents discovered in a tomb in 1975.

Laozi. *Daodejing* (third century B.C.E.). Of the many, many translations of this classic text, we recommend four as particularly fine:

- D. C. Lau, trans. *Lao Tzu: Tao Te Ching*. New York: Penguin, 1963.
- Robert G. Henricks, trans. *Lao-tzu Te-Tao Ching: A New Translation Based on the Recently Discovered Ma-wang-tui Texts*. New York: Ballantine, 1989.
- Victor H. Mair, trans. *Tao Te Ching: The Classic Book of Integrity and the Way*. New York: Bantam Books, 1990.
- Moss Roberts, trans. *Dao De Jing: The Book of the Way*. Berkeley: University of California Press, 2001.

Legge, James, trans. *The Chinese Classics*. 2nd ed. 5 vols. Oxford: Clarendon Press, 1893–1895; reprint, Hong Kong: Hong Kong University Press,

1960. This pioneering, thoroughly annotated Victorian translation of the *Analects*, two chapters from the *Record of Ritual*, the *Book of Songs*, the *Book of Documents*, and the *Spring and Autumn Annals* (with its most important ancient commentary) is still very much worth consulting. In fact, it continues to be the only full English translation of the last two texts.

Shang Yang. *The Book of Lord Shang* (fourth century B.C.E.). J.J.L. Duyvendak, trans. *The Book of Lord Shang: A Classic of the Chinese School of Law*. London: A. Probsthain, 1928.

Sima Qian. *Shiji* (c. 100 B.C.E.).

- Raymond Dawson, trans. *Sima Qian: Historical Records*. The World's Classics Series. New York: Oxford University Press, 1994. Translations of key chapters dealing with the Qin Empire. Very light annotations.

- William H. Nienhauser, Jr., et al. trans. *The Grand Scribe's Records*. 10 vols. projected. Bloomington: Indiana University Press, 1994–present. This will be the first complete translation of the *Shiji* into English. It features extensive annotations and is keyed to the standard Chinese edition.

- Burton Watson, trans. *Records of the Grand Historian, Qin Dynasty* and *Records of the Grand Historian, Han Dynasty*, 2 vols., rev. ed. New York and Hong Kong: *Renditions*-Columbia University Press, 1993. Includes most of the *Shiji* in very readable form, but with almost no footnotes. An earlier edition of the Han volumes in Wade-Giles romanization was published by Columbia University Press in 1961.

Sunzi. *Art of War* (fourth century B.C.E.).

- Samuel B. Griffith, trans. *Sun Tzu: The Art of War*. Oxford: Clarendon Press, 1963.

- Roger T. Ames, trans. *Sun-tzu: The Art of Warfare: A New Translation Incorporating the Recently Discovered Yin-ch'üeh-shan Texts*. New York: Ballantine Books, 1993.

Swann, Nancy Lee. *Food and Money in Ancient China: The Earliest Economic History of China to A.D. 25*. Princeton: Princeton University Press, 1950. An annotated translation of *Han shu*, ch. 24 ("Treatise on Food and Money") and 91 ("Biographies of Money-Makers") and *Shiji*, ch. 129 ("Biographies of Money-makers").

Films

Documentaries

Ancient Civilizations: Ancient China. Written and produced by Lara Lowe. Princeton, NJ: Films for the Humanities & Sciences, 1999. 47 mins. Survey of Chinese philosophy and culture, with about half the program focusing on the Qin and Han dynasties and, in particular, the First Emperor.

China: Heritage of the Wild Dragon. NHK Enterprises; director, Katsuhiro Inoue. Princeton, NJ: Films for the Humanities & Sciences, 2001. 59 mins. This documentary explores Chinese history from Neolithic times to the Qin dynasty, with much attention given to excavated tombs and a fascinating re-creation of a bronze vessel using traditional methods of metal casting.

The Immortal Emperor: Shihuangdi. Princeton, NJ: Films for the Humanities & Sciences, 1996. 46 mins. A video tour with academic commentary of the First Emperor's tomb and the terra-cotta army. The inside of the tomb itself is represented with computer animation.

Legacy: China, the Mandate of Heaven (program 3). Michael Wood, host/writer. New York: Ambrose Video Publishing, 1991. 57 mins. A general introduction to Chinese history and culture. In its treatment of ancient China, it focuses on Confucianism and Daoism.

Feature Films

The Emperor and the Assassin (1999). Directed by Chen Kaige. The climactic event of this film is a famous assassination attempt against the First Emperor. The writer and director add numerous twists to the basic plot as found in the *Shiji*, but the scale of the re-creation of Qin's armies conquering China makes for a remarkable epic, and in 1999, this was indeed the most expensive Chinese film ever made. Rated R.

The Emperor's Shadow (1996). Directed by Zhou Xiaowen. This is a fantasy based on the relationship between the First Emperor and a court musician. Almost everything is fiction, but some of the characters like Zhao Gao, Li Si, and the First Emperor are based on historical figures. And there actually was a musician named Gao Jianli who tried to assassinate the emperor. Not rated.

Farewell, My Concubine (1993). Directed by Chen Kaige. The main storyline follows two celebrated actors of Chinese opera from the 1920s to the 1970s. The title of the film refers to their most celebrated roles in the opera

"Farewell, My Concubine," which re-enacts Xiang Yu's last goodbye to Lady Yu before his defeat at the hands of Liu Bang. There is an interesting interplay between modern Chinese history and events at the beginning of the Han Empire, but be forewarned that the film is fairly grim. Rated R.

Internet Sources

British Museum Compass. This is the British Museum's online database, which includes images of about five thousand objects. Type in "Eastern Zhou," "Qin," or "Han" for color photos and detailed descriptions of significant artifacts that illustrate aspects of life in early China. www.thebritish museum.ac.uk/compass.

China Knowledge. Provides brief overviews of most aspects of Chinese history and culture (and includes Chinese characters for key terms). www.chinak-nowledge.org.

China Resources, Five College Center for East Asian Studies. A joint project by Amherst, Hampshire, Mount Holyoke, and Smith Colleges, and the University of Massachusetts at Amherst, which brings together an extensive catalog of resources available for teachers who wish to incorporate units on China into their curriculum. www.smith.edu/fcceas/china/cc.htm.

Traditions of Exemplary Women: A Bilingual Resource for the Study of Women in Early China. This site is based on the *Lienü zhuan* (Traditions of Exemplary Women) by Liu Xiang (77–6 B.C.E.). It includes a translation of the text, along with enough images, maps, essays, and commentaries to provide a full picture of life for women in early China. www.iath.virginia.edu/xwomen.

Curriculum Guides

Ancient China. Ancient World History Development Team. Palo Alto, CA: Teachers' Curriculum Institute, 1998. This unit encourages student interaction and includes a cassette, slide lecture, and student notebook.

The Concept of Order in Ancient China. Adrian Chan and Richard Chu. Stanford: Stanford Program on International and Cross-Cultural Education, 1996. Beginning with a discussion of the Warring States Era and the Qin Empire, this unit incorporates the study of science, agriculture, government, and the pervasive influence of Confucianism on life in ancient China.

Demystifying the Chinese Language. Bay Area China Education Project. Stanford: Stanford Program on International and Cross-Cultural Education, 1983. This book is a series of exercises that involve students and help them understand the basic principles of the Chinese language. No prior knowledge about Chinese is required of either the teacher or the students to use this unit.

Early Chinese History: The Hundred Schools Period. Clayton Dube and Lehn Huff. Los Angeles: National Center for History in the Schools, 1995. The unit includes background materials for teachers, lesson plans, and student resources about the period, focusing particularly on Confucianism, Mohism, Daoism, and Legalism.

Han China/Ancient Rome: Comparing Two Classical Civilizations. Royce Black. China Institute/Programs for Educators. Activities, background information, and internet resources to help students make meaningful comparisons between two ancient civilizations. Available online: www.chinainstitute. org/educators/curriculum/han/introduction.html

INDEX

Note: references in **bold** are to an individual's biography

About the Authors

GRANT HARDY is Associate Professor of History at the University of North Carolina, Asheville.

ANNE BEHNKE KINNEY is Professor of Chinese, and Director of the East Asia Center at the University of Virginia. As a graduate student she spent two years in the department of History and Archaeology at Peking University. She is the author of *Representations of Childhood and Youth in Early China* (2003), and has published numerous articles and scholarly publications.